About the Content Marketing Institute

The Content Marketing Institute teaches non-media brands how to attract and retain customers through compelling, multi-channel storytelling. CMI does this through multiple offerings including the Content Marketing World event, *Chief Content Officer* magazine, electronic and print books from leading content marketing experts, speaking and workshop engagements, and content marketing consulting services.

Content Marketing Institute books are available at special quantity discounts to use as premiums and sales promotions, or for use in corporate training programs. To place a bulk order, please contact the Content Marketing Institute at info@contentinstitute.com or 888/554-2014.

www.contentmarketinginstitute.com

Library of Congress Control Number: 2012944015

ISBN: 978-0-9833307-8-3

Printed in the United States of America.

ANDREW M. DAVIS

"Gamechanging"
–Steve Rotter, Marketing Vice President & Entrepreneur

Brandscaping

Unleashing the
Power of Partnerships

With Foreword By MarketingProfs'
Ann Handley

To my wife,
whose patience,
understanding, and smile
have made me the success
I am today.

Table of Contents

PART ONE: THE PARADIGM SHIFTS

PART TWO: BRANDING IN THE NEW WORLD

PART THREE: CONTENT IS CURRENCY

Foreword

When Andrew first approached me about writing the foreword to his new book, I reacted with an enthusiastic "yes!" Andrew is a friend and a colleague, and the kind of genuine, *nice-guys-finish-first* person who deserves to succeed. Without even seeing a draft, I said, "I'd love to!"

Then he mentioned the title, and I felt a small rise of panic. On the outside, I played it cool. But inside I was thinking, "*wait… Brandscaping?! This is a book about branding?*" I had assumed that Andrew's book would be about content marketing—a topic I know far more about.

As a former journalist and current chief content officer and business-book author, I am qualified to speak with some authority about various topics in marketing. But just between you and me, I wouldn't put branding at the top of the list, especially when there are so many branding experts out there who could run circles around me when it comes to the topic.

But before I could find the words to graciously back out, Andrew sent his draft. And I relaxed.

Because what you now hold isn't a book about branding in the old-school sense—big advertising budgets and broadcast messaging. Instead, this is a book that talks about how to build a brand in a richly storied world where we have new and interesting ways to connect with our prospects and customers—through (you guessed it) content!

Andrew calls this "brandscaping," or (as he writes) using and treating content as an asset rather than an expense.

I love that, because it's consistent with how I think about content, too: Your ability to publish blogs, and make videos, and post photos to Instagram, and create infographics and slide shows and podcasts and webinars and cartoons and e-books and puppet shows and whatever else you might dream up isn't merely table stakes for getting found by Google search. Instead, your content marketing presents a rich opportunity.

To do what? To connect with your customers and prospects in a meaningful way. To tell your story in a way that draws your customers to you. To resonate more deeply with them. To create something new and interesting with a set of new tools and an array of new channels. To create content that can drive real business growth and, I believe, transform your business.

Does that sound all blue-sky and Kumbaya? It shouldn't. Because that's the real opportunity all brands now have before them. Content *is* what will set your company apart—because it will define how you relate to your customers, and whether your customers choose you over everyone else.

And that's exactly what this book is about. Here, Andrew shows how the most successful companies are embracing content as a cornerstone of marketing, and—more specifically—how they are using it to grow their brands. He spells out how those companies view the opportunity that's before them—and before all of us—as an exciting time for all kinds of businesses.

So how about you?

Don't read this book if you have a million dollars to buy a billboard in Times Square, as Andrew says (a billboard that will, by the way, not have anywhere near the lasting resonance of a well-crafted blog). But if you want to create something far more lasting and meaningful? Welcome to *Brandscaping*.

Ann Handley
Chief Content Officer, MarketingProfs
Co-author, *Content Rules: How to Create Killer Blogs, Podcasts, Videos, Ebooks, Webinars (and More) that Engage Customers and Ignite Your Business* (Wiley, new in paperback 2012)

Introduction

Brand/skāp-ing: A process that brings like-minded brands and their respective audiences together to create content that increases demand and drives revenue.

Should You Read This Book?

Look, if you want to raise awareness for your brand, buy advertising—lots of it. Buy banner ads, Facebook ads, and sponsored tweets. Buy Google Adwords and television commercials. Buy space in magazines and air time on the radio. But realize this: the space you buy isn't permanent, and the time you buy is fleeting.

On the other hand, if you want to increase demand for your products, create content—lots of it. And not just any content, but great content. Great content shows people how your product or service can impact their lives. It gets people to buy your stuff more often—for the right reasons—and leave more satisfied. But creating great content—the right kind of content—isn't easy. You're going to need partners. You're going to have to brandscape.

So, if you want to buy more advertising, don't read this book. It's a huge waste of time and your hard-earned money. There are too many great books out there about everything from developing effective advertising strategies to creating a successful campaign.

So, if you want to raise awareness, go buy ads. If you want to increase demand, this book is for you and it's worth every penny.

A New Methodology

When I first started telling people I was writing a book called *Brandscaping*, I got a lot of blank stares. "Brandscaping?" I was asked. "What's brandscaping?"

The simplest way I can put it, is that brandscaping is a new way of thinking. It's more than a content marketing strategy or a social media initiative. It's a marketing methodology *that enables you to leverage content as an asset instead of treating it as an expense.* This book is going to show you how. There are plenty of examples out there of companies that are brandscaping quite successfully, and you're going to learn about several of them right here.

Did you know that companies just like yours spend more than $8 billion a year on PR initiatives just so they can get some type of brief coverage about their products and services in a magazine, on a TV show, by a blogger or a newspaper reporter? Even worse, companies spend another $600 billion worldwide on advertising that is, for the most part, ignored.

What if you invested that money in creating content that consumers actually want to consume? On content that would solidify your relationship with the audience you already have and attract the new audiences you want? Content itself is an investment—it's something you own, not something fleeting like a press mention or a TV commercial.

Brandscaping hinges on creating relevant, frequently delivered, compelling content that engages, inspires, and informs your audience—just like the media companies of old. Except, in a brandscaper's world, you don't have to rely on the media alone for access to your audience. You don't have to rely on traditional journalists to write stories and magazines to publish them. You don't need television and radio stations to produce shows, or professional photographers to shoot images. In a brandscaper's world, you forge content relationships, pool your financial and media resources, and share your audience with those who have something to offer. In return, you get access to their audiences, too.

Ever thought of yourself as a talent scout or a media executive? Brandscaping turns you into one. It allows you to tap into trends, target multiple niches, and create movements. Brandscapers don't focus on becoming publishers; they focus on letting others create content for their existing audiences.

Pooling resources—your audience, your expertise, and your money— with other brands that value the same prospects and customers makes your marketing dollars go further. In most cases, you can get more content for the same amount you would spend on traditional advertising and PR and produce a greater return on investment.

Brandscaping is the first marketing methodology to take advantage of monumental shifts in the media industry, social media, publishing, advertising, and PR. To be a successful brandscaper, you have to understand the changes in the media landscape, buy-in to the value of editorially sound content, borrow the best content creation methods, leverage the power of your brand, and choose the best distribution tactics to better serve your audience. In the end, you'll have a more loyal customer base, a higher-quality customer acquisition strategy, and a more powerful and successful sales engine—overall, a better brand.

To be a successful brandscaper you need three things:

- The *confidence* to invest in the content of others and the belief that their audience, no matter how small, is valuable.
- The *humility* to believe that your customers care about more than just *your* products and services.
- The *willingness* to pool your resources and share your audience with other brands to make your marketing budget go farther.

You may not be willing to embrace these ideas right now, but by the end of the book you should be.

From Taxi Dispatcher to Makeup Mogul

Let me start by sharing one of my favorite examples of brandscaping at work.

In 2007, Lauren Luke began selling make-up products on eBay in an effort to subsidize her income as a taxi dispatcher in Newcastle, England. To improve her sales, Lauren decided to start creating practical, makeup application videos on YouTube. Some of her most popular videos featured her step-by-step instructions on recreating celebrity looks.

For example, Lauren noticed the unique makeup stylings of Britney Spears in her music video for *Toxic*, so she created a tutorial video so fans could mimic the look at home. The 10-minute video isn't over-produced, and as the *New York Times* pointed out, "with her plump proportions and pretty if nondescript features, she seems an unlikely candidate to shake up the beauty world."

"There are no expensive edits. There's no polish. People crave real. They don't want spectacular effects and models," Lauren says. Lauren's content is unbelievably authentic and it works. Lauren's Britney Spears video has over 1.6 million views and that's not her most successful content to date. Some of her videos have been viewed more than 4 million times and, in total, her content has garnered over 111 million views. How many video views does Estee Lauder have on YouTube? Last time I checked, fewer than 150,000. Lauren's content is 100 times more successful than one of the world's largest beauty brands.

Lauren became a prolific YouTube content creator, posting at least one or two videos a week. In 2009, advertising agency Anomaly took note.

Essentially, Anomaly understood the power of the content Lauren had been creating and the audience she'd garnered. Instead of marketing her as a spokesperson for Estee Lauder or MAC, Anomaly partnered (and invested) in helping Lauren launch her own make-up line without a dollar of traditional advertising attached. As the partnership evolved, and in an effort to secure retail distribution for the new line of makeup called By Lauren Luke, the Anomaly team approached the make-up retail giant Sephora.

Before long, By Lauren Luke was on store shelves at Sephora, right down the aisle from beauty brands that spend hundreds-of-millions of dollars on traditional advertising and marketing. And it all started with a solid content strategy. Lauren's insight and advice to an audience of women hoping to emulate a celebrity make-up look built up the demand for her own make-up line.

Lauren + Anomaly + Sephora = a brandscape

Lauren expanded her brandscape, almost continuously finding new opportunities to partner with others. In 2009, she released a line of printed books (yes, printed) titled *Looks by Lauren Luke* in a partnership with British publishing house Hodder & Stoughton. A month later, she debuted as an avatar in the Nintendo DS video game *Supermodel Makeover By Lauren Luke*.

Sephora, Nintendo, and even a traditional book publisher are leveraging Lauren's simple content concept to increase demand for their respective products. Meanwhile, the books, the make-up line, the Nintendo game, and Lauren's content all help sell each other's products.

To take it a step further, Lauren leverages celebrity brands by customizing her content to appeal to niches within her core group. "If I do a video inspired by looks from the popular book series *Twilight*, I can grab hold of the *Twilight* audience. But if I do a Kelly Clarkson-inspired look, I can tap into a totally different audience," Lauren explains.

Today, by her own estimation, the Lauren Luke brand is worth more than $100 million and it all started with focused, niche content on YouTube. This is what happens when you brandscape.

Brandscaping: A Mall for Your Marketing

Have you ever thought about why you like to shop at your favorite mall? Is it because all your favorite stores are there? Let me tell you a little secret: Every shopping center is an intentionally crafted brandscape designed to increase demand for all of the products and services sold there. That's the power of brandscaping—working with others to increase demand for every partner's product.

There's a science behind shopping malls. You have to have the right tenant mix. You have to understand the market your mall will serve and the competition near by. You have to pick the right anchor tenants. You even have to understand how each tenant adds value to your shopper's experience.

Brandscaping is no different. To be a successful brandscaper, you have to think more like a mall developer than a marketer, advertiser, or public relations person.

Anchor tenants define a mall's success. Nordstrom's, Sears, J.C. Penney, Target, Kmart, Costco, Home Depot, Walmart, and Bloomingdales are all very different brands. These brands set the tone for the mall experience. They attract specific types of consumers, as well as certain types of smaller tenants that are going after those specific types of consumers.

A mall anchored by Whole Foods might attract brands like Lulu Lemon, Nike, L.L. Bean, and restaurants such as P.F. Chang's and The Cheesecake Factory, because they all target the same customer. On the other hand, a mall anchored by Kmart might attract brands like Bed, Bath & Beyond, Staples, and PetSmart, and restaurants such as Chuck E. Cheese and Panera.

The right kind of tenant mix means you attract the right kind of customers with the right frequency for the right reasons. The right tenant mix means your customers will stay longer and spend more. In fact, the success of any retail development hinges on every brand leveraging the success of every other store for their mutual gain. In essence, a rising tide lifts all ships.

Here's how the science affects shopping behavior: I might visit Whole Foods every two weeks. If Whole Foods is next to L.L. Bean, I might stop there to buy a jacket. If I get hungry while I'm at L.L. Bean, I might walk over to The Cheesecake Factory for lunch. After lunch I might go to a movie, or stop in the Apple Store for an accessory. I might go into one of the gift shops to buy a birthday gift, or browse a sale at a boutique clothing store.

If Whole Foods was alone in a parking lot instead of a shopping center, I never would have gone to all these other stores. I would have gone home, unloaded my groceries and called it a chore. Instead, it was an experience. An experience where I spent more, stayed longer, and interacted with brands I hadn't planned on visiting when I set out that morning.

The web is filled with billions of shopping malls, except these malls aren't filled with products. They're full of content. Content like Lauren Luke's. Lauren's content created an anchor tenant for millions of teenage girls looking for make-up advice. They visited her content every couple of weeks and before Lauren realized it, she'd garnered a loyal, high-quality audience that was valuable to other brands. Sephora, Nintendo, the book publisher and, of course, Lauren Luke's make-up line are the other "stores" that round-out a consumer's Lauren Luke experience. Lauren built a valuable little mall in the digital world.

Why You Need to Read this Book

Odds are you aren't going to hear about the power of brandscaping from your ad agency or your PR firm. You certainly aren't going to hear about it from your media partners or your trusty trade magazine. You aren't going to learn about how to work with other brands or new talent from your digital agency who's spending your cash on umpteen Google Adwords either.

None of these partners are going to help you build a portfolio of content creators that's designed to drive sales with niche audiences for one simple reason: it undermines their existing business models.

How to Read this Book

There are millions of marketing how-to books on the market. This isn't a how-to book. This is a how-to *think* book.

There are too many things to learn in a digital marketing landscape. You're supposed to know how to use LinkedIn to drive business…how to build a successful blog…how to promote your products using Google Adwords…the list goes on and on. It's overwhelming.

But you know what? You don't have to learn any of those things. There are people you can hire who know that stuff. You can also leverage partners in your brandscape who already do these things better than you.

What you *do* need to learn is how to think about the digital landscape. You need to think about why you're on LinkedIn (or Twitter, or YouTube, or Facebook). You need to think about what's on your blog—or whether you should even have one. You need to figure out the best ways to introduce your products and services to new prospects and attract a bigger audience.

So while you're reading this book, I want you to be thinking—not about how to push buttons, but about new ways of doing things… about ways you can partner with others to build a stronger brand.

Asking the Right Questions

This book is full of stories, case studies, and marketing lessons. But more importantly, it's designed to help you ask the right questions.

Over the last decade, I've worked with hundreds of companies to help them build successful digital strategies and if I've learned one thing, it's that most mistakes and missteps are *not* the result of implementing the wrong tactics—they're the result of asking the wrong questions.

If you ask the wrong question, even when the answer's right, you cannot be successful. It's the difference between asking how to get from point A to point B instead of asking what's the fastest way to get from point A to point B. You still might arrive, but you'll quite possibly be late.

Every business is different. The tactics you implement should be different. Even your strategies will seem wildly different. However, the questions you should be asking are the same.

That's why you'll see sidebars in this book titled Ask Yourself. These questions are designed to challenge your marketing and sales teams. These are the questions that you need to keep reminding yourself of. The questions you should be asking your CEO and your business partners. The questions your employees, customers, clients, and even prospects can help answer. If you're going to be successful in the digital world, you must consistently question every move.

A Word About Video

We live in a world where content can transcend media faster than ever before. Great blogs can become best-selling books. Best-selling books can become movies. YouTube video creators have become music icons like Justin Bieber. Ideas hatched on Twitter have become sitcoms. There's a digital content continuum that enables successful content on one media to be translated to another at an ever-increasing pace.

Today, every single one of my clients wants a "video strategy." They want to know how to get people to watch the content they create on Vimeo, LiveStream, or YouTube. I started out in television and film, so I'm comfortable building digital strategies that include video, and we've been successful doing that. However, the same strategies that build a successful YouTube audience can also be used to build a blog following, or a valuable audience of Facebook fans.

The point is, don't fall into one of the most basic digital traps. Don't assume that because it works in one media or online channel it can't work on another. This book is full of success stories that leverage video as a marketing and brandscaping strategy. But every one of these case studies could be executed as a podcast, a blog, or even a book. In the digital world, you must focus on using the right media for the right content delivered at the right time.

With every example in this book, I want you to constantly question the media being used. Ask yourself: if this wasn't produced as video, could it work as a blog post, or start as a Tweet stream? Would this work as a podcast or a set of images?

What If?

I'm a believer in thinking big. The bigger you think, the stronger your vision and conviction. Too many marketers stop just short of a big success because they aren't constantly asking themselves one simple question: What if?

That's exactly what IBM has done numerous times and it's come to define their brand.

IBM has long been respected as one of the most powerful business solutions providers in the marketplace. Sure, they've done tons of traditional advertising, but IBM also has a track record of embracing brandscaping, even before the age of social media and the web revolution.

In 1997, IBM had spent six years working to build a computer that could beat a world-champion chess player. IBM's efforts paid off when Deep Blue, its chess-playing computer, beat famed chess player Gary Kasparov. Immediately, IBM had positioned itself as a problem-solver, able to tackle even the most complex problems and succeed.

In addition, the game of chess and even Gary Kasparov were propelled into the national spotlight. Essentially, IBM enlisted the brands of Gary Kasparov, the game of chess, and the clever concept of an insurmountable brand challenge to create some of the most compelling content in modern public relations history. The message: if you have a business challenge to solve, IBM will do it.

IBM had asked one simple question: What if a computer could beat a human at chess?

In 2011, IBM did it again, except this time they partnered with the game show *Jeopardy*.

It all started in 2004 when a team of IBM employees, led by IBM researcher Charles Lickel, set out to build a machine that could beat Ken Jennings, who had won the most *Jeopardy* games in the show's history.

IBM documented the entire process on video. They videotaped the failures, the small successes, and even the practice rounds where their computer answered *Jeopardy* questions with answers that showed how complicated the logic was. IBM named the computer Watson.

On Valentine's Day 2011, Watson took the stage to compete for two consecutive nights against Ken Jennings and Brad Butler, another highly successful *Jeopardy* contestant.

On the first night, *Jeopardy's* ratings skyrocketed to 14.5 million viewers, 24 percent higher than the same day a year before. By the second night, given all the media coverage and online buzz leading into the evening's show, *Jeopardy* outperformed every show on TV in the top 10 television markets. Over the course of two days, more than 30 million viewers tuned-in to watch Watson take the *Jeopardy Challenge* and win!

But *Jeopardy* wasn't the only one with positive results to tout.

IBM, in its quarterly earnings report, attributed the 20 percent growth in its analytics business for the quarter to the remarkable success of Watson on *Jeopardy*. Even IBM's chief financial officer, Mark Loughridge, described Watson's triumph as a calculated marketing move designed to drive revenue. "We didn't invest just to play *Jeopardy*, we invested to prove leadership applications for our clients."

In a media marketplace dominated by brands like Apple, Google, and Facebook, IBM proved once again that it was one of the most innovative technology players in the marketplace.

IBM had asked one more simple question: What if a computer could beat a human at *Jeopardy*?

Good marketers and great brandscapers are always asking "What if?" What if we thought a little bigger? What if we made one more strategic connection? What if we took one more step, did one more thing, had one more conversation?

Every chapter in *Brandscaping* includes a section called "What if." These sections are designed to help you explore the additional untapped opportunities for the case studies in this book.

It wasn't easy for IBM to build Watson. But they documented every misstep. Those missteps and challenges turned into a PBS special on NOVA called "The Smartest Machine on Earth" (another brandscape). Those missteps showed how IBM thinks. How they solve problems. How they succeed, no matter how big the challenge.

As a business professional, asking yourself "What if?" will challenge your team to rise to the challenge, to rally around a big idea. A big idea that has the power to transform your business, even your industry.

Part One
The Paradigm Shifts

Marketing is broken. Social media won't save it. Online ads won't reinvent themselves. Google's acquiring. Public relations is changing. The music industry is reinventing itself. The movie business is struggling. Newspapers are dying. Your email inbox is full. Your mobile device is always on. Your DVR is recording. Your iPad apps are updating. I don't need to tell you that the media business is in flux.

If you're going to survive in a world where everything's changing, you're going to have to think differently. You're going to have to:

- Break down the barriers between corporate communications, product development, branding, and public relations.
- Find new ways to work with your spokespeople, your customer service team, and your account managers.
- Ask more from your media partners and advertising channels.
- Find new ways to interact with your influencers and embrace your loyal customers.
- Explore innovative ways to test, develop, and promote your products.
- Rethink the way you access a valuable audience.
- Find new customers, fans, and followers.
- Increase margins by relying less on promotions, sales, and group discounts to drive revenue.

You need more than new marketing tactics to survive. You need a new marketing philosophy.

Chapter 1
Embracing the Idea of Increasing Demand

Awareness or Demand? You Choose

As a marketer or business owner, you've been trained to think about raising awareness for the products and services you sell. You've read advertising books and attended online seminars that have told you how to position your products and write effective calls to action. You've advertised in magazines and newspapers. You've worked hard to make your company visible in the marketplace.

But did you ever stop to think how you could raise *demand* for your products and services?

"I Want a Nemo!"

In 2003, Disney and the talented team at Pixar released the animated film, *Finding Nemo*. The movie followed a desperate clownfish in search of his son, stolen from their coral reef. The underwater adventure tracks Nemo's shy father all the way from their home on the Great Barrier Reef to the hustle and bustle of Sydney Harbor.

As families watched the movie, demand for pet clownfish increased. "Parents whose children fell in love with Nemo at the cinema are seeking out the clownfish in ever greater numbers, leading to over-harvesting of wild specimens because captive breeding programs cannot cope with demand," said Hannah Strange, an environmental reporter for *Times Online*.[1]

Scientists actually determined that in less than one year, *Finding Nemo* had contributed to a precipitous fall in the global population of clownfish. They even named the "environmental impact that a media property can propagate in the wild" the *Nemo Effect*.

This wasn't the first time Disney had inadvertently caused a run on pets. In 1961, consumer demand for dalmations rose when Disney released the film *101 Dalmatians*.[2]

Finding Nemo is evergreen. Nine years after the movie's debut, I can still buy a *Finding Nemo*-branded aquarium at Walmart for thirty bucks.

Think about this for a moment: *Finding Nemo* and *101 Dalmatians* increased demand for fish and dogs.

What kind of advertising budget would you have to tap to create a demand large enough to deplete the global population of clownfish? What would that campaign look like? Would it even work?

A Rising Tide Lifts All Ships

Finding Nemo caused millions of kids to fall in love with the idea of having a fish. Pet stores sold more aquariums, more clownfish, more goldfish, and even more Chinese fighting fish. They sold more fish food, more gravel, more pumps, and even more goods completely unrelated to fish.

Disney boosted an entire industry with the release of one film. *Finding Nemo* was the tide that lifted all ships. As children began asking for their own aquariums, nearly everyone in the aquatic pet industry saw an increase in sales.

In the advertising world, the fish food manufacturer would have spent its own ad dollars espousing the virtues of its brand. The aquarium manufacturer would have spent money telling you why its fish tank is better than the rest. The pet store would have advertised specials and sent out flyers with coupons to try to get you in the door. Even with all of their individual efforts, they wouldn't have convinced more families to buy fish.

This is the problem with most marketing strategies today. You're worried about your market share in the fish food space or the aquarium market. You're worried if your fish tank is selling more than another brand of fish tank. Meanwhile, fewer and fewer people are inspired to buy fish.

If your market's getting smaller but your market share remains the same, are you making more money? No—you're making less.

The inverse is also true. You can try to convince consumers to switch to your brand of fish food, but this is expensive and extremely difficult. (They already like another brand.) Or, you can focus on getting more people to buy fish.

If your market's getting bigger, even while your market share remains the same, are you making more money? Yes.

Smart brandscapers look for opportunities to make long-term plays that increase the size of the market itself. The more you're involved in increasing the size of your market (rising the tide), the more prepared you are to capitalize on its growth. That's when you start stealing market share.

Imagine if the aquarium manufacturer, the fish food company, the clownfish farmer, the gravel supplier, and the pet store all pooled their marketing resources to drive demand for pet fish. Imagine if they thought more like Disney and less like individual brand marketers. Their marketing dollars would go farther and they'd all sell more product.

Imagine if *you* started to focus your marketing efforts on pooling your resources with other like-minded companies to move your market. *Your* marketing dollars would go farther, *you* would reach more people, and *you* would end up selling more. A good brandscaper focuses on one simple mantra: a rising tide lifts all ships.

So stop thinking about your brand in a vacuum and start looking for opportunities to increase the size of your market.

WHAT IF...

Imagine, for a minute, that the pet store industry embraced the simple idea that a rising tide lifts all ships. What if pet stores capitalized on the opportunity to create content, like Disney, to increase demand for the animals (and all the ancillary products) they sell? First, let's look at the math and find the pooled resources to create brandscaped content.

There are approximately 8,700 pet stores in the United States. Assume that a pet industry association invited every pet store to contribute $1,000 every year toward a brandscaping initiative. Suddenly, their pooled resources total $8.7 million! Now, that's only 10 percent of the budget Disney and Pixar raised for *Finding Nemo*, but the pet stores don't need $87 million to create short-form video content for a weekly online series. Their $8 million will be just fine.

With a weekly budget of $163,000, the pet industry could create an amazingly high-quality, entertaining, even educational, kids show designed specifically to endear children to a specific set of characters just like Nemo. Characters that map directly to the kind of pets and pet products these stores want to sell.

In fact, here's an idea: In 2001, the British Broadcasting Corporation (BBC) released an adult-oriented situation comedy called Pets. The 11-minute program followed the everyday lives of four anthropomorphic animals (played by a set of puppets) living in a London apartment. The show took a very simple premise and turned it into an entertaining, if raunchy, look at the lives of our pets when humans leave the house for the day.

What if the pet industry took the same premise and turned it into a kids-oriented children's series and released it every week on YouTube or as a web series on Netflix or iTunes?

Pets wasn't a breakout success. The show aired late at night and was targeted at an adult audience. While it did garner a cult following for the 26 episodes that BBC produced, it was shot, edited, and created for a miniscule budget of about $10,000 per episode. Imagine what you could do with a budget 10 times that size?

What if the pet industry embraced the idea that content like *Finding Nemo* sells more fish?

What if *your* industry association embraced the simple idea that a rising tide lifts all ships? What if they helped pull together the resources you need to increase demand for the products you sell?

This is how brandscapers think.

Ask Yourself...

What products or services do our customers buy before they have a need for our wares?

To drive demand in your product category, you have to investigate the product brandscape that triggers the need for your company's solutions.

If you sell accounting software, what do consumers buy *before* they realize they need a software solution? Do they buy a basic accounting book? Do they purchase a computer and a printer? Do they lease office space? What if you helped those types of companies drive interest in their products and services?

Millions of families that bought a ticket to see *Finding Nemo* or watched it on DVD ended up in a pet store. What if you were an aquarium pump manufacturer and you got more people to watch *Finding Nemo*? What if you helped drive traffic into pet stores? Don't you think you'd sell more pumps?

The more people purchase your brandscape partners' products, the more you'll drive demand for yours.

Chapter 2
Content Sells Stuff

Looking at the Past Defines the Future

Brandscaping is a hybrid marketing model that blends the best and still relevant advertising and PR strategies with newer tactics—such as custom publishing, underwriting, social media, and content marketing—to leverage the power of the new media world we live in.

There are plenty of marketing experts who will tell you the marketing landscape has changed. Most of these experts are looking forward, trying to predict the next big thing and how it will forever change the way you market your business and how to leverage it for your company's gain. However, very few people are looking back at our rich, innovative, and fascinating media history to understand what worked in the past and why—and whether it might still be relevant today.

The Soap Opera

Brandscaping, custom publishing, and even content marketing's origins can be traced back to Chicago in the early 1930s when an entrepreneurial radio station manager approached a margarine manufacturer with a proposal for a new kind of program. The program, written by a woman named Irna Phillips, was a 15-minute serialized drama called *Painted Dreams*. The show featured the morning conversations between a mother, her daughter, and their female boarder before the two young women went off to work at a hotel in town.

The program's goal was to marry the needs of the margarine manufacturer (and later a detergent manufacturer) to the listening interests of its target audience: women between the ages of 18 and 49. *Painted Dreams* was a success. Soon after, stations around the country started selling and producing what became known as "soap operas."

Soap operas became so successful in generating loyal, high-quality, target audiences that by 1940, soaps accounted for 60 percent of all radio revenue. Irna Phillips was the highest-paid radio scriptwriter in the nation, making the equivalent of $3.2 million per year.

During that same year, Procter & Gamble (P&G) created its own soap opera production subsidiary, P&G Productions, which went on to produce the world's first television soap opera. By 1960, daytime television was attracting millions of female viewers each day.

Let's break this down. P&G, a company that sells household cleaning supplies, launched a media production company to create content for a specific audience with the clear understanding that it would result in greater sales. P&G Productions still exists today, although it's getting out of the soap opera business, investing in digital content, and moving into more "family-friendly programming."

If there's one thing we can learn from Irna Phillips and the soap opera empire she created, it's that the content we create "must actually sell merchandise," as she famously said. Irna had no illusions about the dramas she wrote. Her 15-minute cliffhangers kept audiences coming back day after day and helped brands like P&G deliver their message to a captive, high-quality audience. The brands that paid for the content creation became household names and largely, perhaps single-handedly, contributed to what P&G is today.

The right content, delivered on the right channel, at the right time, to the right people, can increase demand for whatever you sell. With *Painted Dreams*, Irna Phillips captured her audience's attention and built her underwriter's brand. The show itself didn't have anything to do with P&G's margarine or soap, yet it effectively sold those products.

To be a successful content creator like Irna, you need to create content that your audience wants and needs. Oftentimes, that content will have little to do with the actual products you sell and more to do with the audience you're looking to attract.

The Modern Soap

Soap operas don't attract the large audiences they did decades ago for one simple reason: the media landscape is so fragmented that it's almost impossible to create one program that will attract the 18 to 49-year-old female demographic anymore. In today's marketplace, you might need five very different programs on five different media channels to reach that very same audience.

But that doesn't mean the soap opera is dead—it's evolving. When Kmart executives decided they wanted to target teens and tweens to showcase a fashion-forward, back-to-school collection, they teamed up with a production company called Alloy Media. Instead of creating an advertising campaign and buying media on television networks and in teen magazines, Kmart and Alloy created a modern-day version of the tried-and-true soap opera.

The original comedy, called *First Day*, followed one girl as she repeated her first day of school over and over again (think *Groundhog Day* meets ABC's Movie of the Week). The 10-minute episodes weren't distributed on Saturday morning television—they were released biweekly on YouTube. They were promoted on Facebook, garnering tens of thousands of fans and hundreds of thousands of views. Kmart's role was summed up simply in the underwriting of the show's title: *First Day*, styled by Kmart. (Of course, Kmart enabled viewers to buy the prepackaged styles showcased in the show at its website, and encouraged viewers to "get the look" and "shop the styles").

"The web series *First Day* proved a hit with tween and teen consumers and succeeded in delivering a dynamic digital experience that resonated with our target consumers during the pivotal back-to-school season," says Andrew Stein, vice president of marketing planning at Sears Holdings (which owns Kmart). It "appeals to their ever-changing media tastes and through an innovative and highly entertaining vehicle that truly hits the mark with this discerning and influential audience," he continues.[3]

The show's first season was a huge success, reaching more than 10 million teen girls. In fact, it was so successful that Kmart invested in a second season, using the same cast of characters, in a series called *First Day 2: First Dance*.

Kmart didn't need hundreds of millions of views—it needed highly influential and engaged school fashionistas to watch the show and buy the looks. It worked.

"First Day resulted in an incredible following, taking our fashion directly to the tween and teen customer," says Tara Poseley, president of apparel at Kmart. "Our ability to create a script with Alloy that was specifically designed to bring our brands to life through the characters and storyline was key to last year's [2010's] success."

So as you can see, the soap opera is alive and well. It has morphed to the point where any brand can create the right kind of content for a niche-focused audience, without a television or radio network, and still reap the benefits of a loyal audience relationship. Clearly, Kmart wouldn't have continued the initiative if it didn't drive demand.

First Day and *First Dance* followed Irna Phillips' first lesson of brandscaping success: your content must actually sell merchandise.

WHAT IF...

What if Irna Phillips were alive today (she died in 1973 at the age of 72)? What if Kmart asked her to apply her skills as a soap opera writer to leverage the power of new media to introduce a new generation to the soap opera in a more relevant and contemporary form?

Irna Phillips would immediately put her time and effort into writing and creating cell-phone novels. That's right, cell-phone novels. Like the soap opera of yesteryear, cell-phone novels are serialized stories tapped out on an author's cell phone and read like text messages by the author's fan base on a daily or weekly basis. They're unedited and unfiltered, and with new chapters (some as short as 200 words) sent straight to your mobile device, they deliver the very same cliffhangers Irna believed drove a consistent and valuable audience for the radio soaps she pioneered.

"What is so attractive for readers about cell-phone novels is that they are [written] in short chapters on an ongoing basis like a continuing TV series, keeping readers craving more...emphasizing dialogue, emotions, and drama," says Satoshi Takatsu, a cell-phone novelist.[4] That sounds exactly like the kind of thing Irna would have embraced.

Cell-phone novels have been around in Asia since 2000, but it wasn't until 2007 that they really hit the mainstream. That's when five of the year's top 10 best-selling printed books in Japan were originally written on a cell phone.

Many cell-phone novels are written by women in their teens or early twenties and they read more like diaries than traditional novels. Rin, number five on the list of Japan's best-selling authors, sold 400,000 copies of the printed version of her book, *If You*, after she typed it out on her phone over the course of her senior year in high school.

If Irna Phillips were around today, she'd scour the digital universe looking for budding cell-phone novelists to partner with. She'd connect them with forward-thinking brands interested in building long-term relationships with an audience—just like she did with the soap operas of the 1930s.

Irna Phillips wouldn't see the soap opera as dead, she would seek out the opportunities to attract a new audience on a new media.

What if you thought like a cell phone-novelist? What if you thought like Irna Phillips?

Ask Yourself...

What content does our audience already have a relationship with and how can our brand embrace it?

Soap operas didn't have anything to do with selling soap. They had everything to do with driving sales by leveraging the long-term relationship the content had with the audience who would *buy* soap.

Diving deep into your audience's content consumption habits will help you reveal the content synergies and potential partnerships that can drive your sales through existing content.

Make a list of all the content (not just websites, but specific content) your audience loves to consume on a regular basis. Include content they've shared and embraced in the past. How can you leverage relationships with this content to build your brand?

Chapter 3
The Downfall of Advertising

The Secret Rule

There's an unwritten rule that advertising agencies and media buyers have held close to their chests for more than 70 years. It's a formula that's lined their pockets with billions of dollars and led to success for many of their clients. It's a simple rule—a rule of proportions. It's called the **90/10 Rule.**

The 90/10 Rule says that you should spend 90 percent of your campaign budget distributing your content and 10 percent crafting, creating, and producing the message. For a $1,000 advertising campaign, that would mean spending $900 for airtime, magazine space, or website impressions, and only $100 on the content in the advertisement that your audience will see or hear.

Today, the 90/10 rule is dead. Everything has changed. The market has shifted. The paradigm for content distribution has flipped in your favor and very few, if any, marketers are taking advantage of the content distribution opportunities afforded to them in the new media world. The rule of advertising proportions has changed.

In today's web world, anyone can attract an audience. Media companies no longer control access to your audience. Distribution is free. People just like you—and the companies you work for—are building their own audiences everyday.

You don't need a newspaper or a magazine to publish your articles, you can start a blog. You don't need to run commercials on TV to attract valuable viewers, just launch a YouTube channel. You don't need a radio station to build an army of listeners, just create a podcast or join BlogTalkRadio. You don't even need a movie deal to distribute your film—you can stream it on Netflix.

Facebook fans, Twitter followers, YouTube subscribers, podcast listeners, Instagrammers, blog readers, eBook buyers, email newsletter recipients—they're all valuable audiences, and they're all owned by you, a competitor and, most certainly, a potential brandscaping partner.

In this new media world, you shouldn't be spending 90 percent of your marketing budget for time and space that you can get for free on the web. You should be spending that money on owning your audience by creating the right kind of content. Content that drives demand.

You need a new rule of proportions. A new secret that relies on the quality of the content you create and the audience you're constantly developing. You need a new formula for success that drives sales, repeat customers, and loyal brand advocates. You need a new law of marketing proportions that spends more on the quality of content you create and less on content distribution. You need to start brandscaping.

The Death of Display Ads

When's the last time you clicked on a banner ad? Seriously.

Over the last 15 years, consumers have trained themselves to ignore digital ads and look for content, a condition called "banner ad blindness." As digital advertising becomes even less effective, marketers will be forced to find new ways to capture their target audience's attention. Slowly but surely, banner ads will be replaced by brandscaping, which is more valuable to the media, the brands creating the content, and the talent behind it.

There's no doubt that the rise of digital media has caused a sea-change in the advertising world. Entire business models have sprung up that make digital advertising accessible to any business, anywhere in the world. For pennies, you can create an advertising campaign on Google, measure its impact, and even adjust the messaging on the fly. But can this business model really last? I'm not so sure, given my understanding of economics fundamentals.

I'm no economist, but any eleventh grade economics teacher can help you understand the simple laws of supply and demand. Essentially, those laws state that as the supply for any commodity increases and the demand remains unchanged (or even decreases), it leads to a lower price for the commodity (with a higher quantity left unpurchased). Obviously, the inverse is true as well. As the commodity becomes more scarce and demand remains unchanged (or even increases), the price of the commodity rises. Of course, if the supply of any commodity outpaces the growth for demand, the price also drops—and so does its value to you.

Imagine if the nearest mile-long strip of highway near your home suddenly had hundreds of billboards lining the road. By law, no strip of interstate freeway can have more than 36 billboards in one mile. That's about one billboard every 136 feet. Let's say that overnight that number jumped to 200 billboards, or one every 26 feet. Those original 36 billboards would be almost impossible to find. As you drove by, all 200 billboards would blend into the scenery, and you'd become "billboard-blind." That's exactly what's happening to digital advertising.

So let's apply these simple laws of supply and demand to digital advertising. Let's take one website, Wordpress.com, and look at the advertising opportunities available.

Wordpress is a complete content management system. Although Wordpress was originally conceived of as a blogging platform, hundreds of thousands of companies have used it to build their websites.

In June 2012, bloggers created an average of 631 new web pages per minute on Wordpress.com. That's 918,277 new web pages in 24 hours. Let's assume there were six new places to advertise on each of those freshly minted web pages. That means there were 5.5 million new places to advertise just on Wordpress.com every single day. In one year, that equated to almost 2 billion new advertising opportunities on one web publishing platform. That's a huge increase in supply.

Google estimates there are tens of billions of new web pages published every day. That means there are hundreds of billions of new places to advertise, too.

As an advertiser, this sounds like a good thing. Lower-priced advertising opportunities mean that you can buy more for your money, right? Sure—with two major exceptions: One, the advertising itself is becoming less effective because with an increased supply it's getting easier to ignore. Two, your audience is becoming more fragmented over a wider selection of content, and it's getting harder to effectively find and target your prospects.

When banner ads first debuted on the web in 1994, those early advertisements garnered high click-through rates (CTR). In fact, the very first one by AT&T generated a 78 percent CTR. That means for every 1,000 people who saw the ad, 780 of them clicked through.

Today, the industry standard for a decent banner ad campaign CTR is .02 percent. That means for every 1,000 people who see the ad, only 20 of them click through. And ironically, the larger the destination, the more banner advertising one sees and the less effective it is.

Media companies, buyers, and agencies know all this, but they've been slow to react. Therefore, you need to take back control of your advertising dollars to ensure that your money is driving your business objectives in a more meaningful way. It no longer makes sense to spend 90 percent of your budget on time or space that you don't own, in a world where consumers are ignoring ads and demanding more content.

A Content Marriage Instead of a One-Night Stand

Today, your marketing efforts are probably characterized by a series of campaigns designed to drive spikes of interest that result in sales or leads. In other words, your marketing efforts are a series of expensive, fun, albeit potentially successful, one-night stands.

Instead, envision a world in which you focus on building long-term, authentic relationships with your media partners, loyal customers, bloggers, podcasters, videographers, talented content creators, other brands, and even your competitors—relationships that make your products relevant in a deeper way. In this scenario, your marketing efforts will look more like a first date that blossoms into a marriage.

However, as with a marriage, you'll have to choose your marketing partners carefully. While digital media has dramatically shifted the marketing landscape, many marketing services providers have not adjusted. The largest shifts have occurred in the advertising, public relations, talent management, and publishing worlds, and to be frank, many of these players haven't figured out how to take advantage of the new opportunities. The good news is you can use this slow movement to your advantage. The bad news is you're going to have to work a little harder to find the right partners to make it happen.

Blendtec, IBM, and Ford are examples of companies that have successfully taken back control of their marketing budgets and leveraged the shifting marketplace with outstanding results. I'm going to show you how to do the same thing. By the time you're finished reading this book, you're going to know how to make your marketing more cost-effective, less campaign-driven, and much more powerful.

Every Brand is a Media Company

We live in a world where anyone can build an audience of passionate, opt-in consumers willing to devour their content. Many attribute the lower barriers to entry for creating content to this phenomenal shift, but in fact, it's the extremely low content distribution barriers that have turned your organization, its employees, and even your customers into media companies.

Decades ago, most companies created relatively little content. It wasn't because creating content was hard or too expensive. In fact, creating content might have been just as easy as it is today. Anyone could write a novel, take amazing photos, even shoot a film on old-fashioned videotape, but there were only two ways to get your content in the hands of consumers: advertising or traditional media channels. If you didn't have a lot of money to spend on advertising, it was nearly impossible to generate an audience.

Back then, traditional marketing consisted of a public relations strategy, an advertising and media buying budget, and the occasional hiring of a spokesperson to raise awareness of your products or services. Today, both an independent consultant and a multi-billion dollar consulting firm can harness the same distribution channels to grow and maintain an audience for the content they create. This is a complete paradigm shift.

Take Adidas, the German shoe and sportswear manufacturer, for example. Adidas has enticed 11 million consumers to subscribe to its content on Facebook by publishing a constant stream of videos, imagery, and insight that keeps its fans coming back. Its audience is about 3 million viewers *larger* than the audience that tuned-in to a 2011 NBA Semi-conference Playoff Game on ESPN. That qualifies Adidas as a media company in my book.

I know what you're thinking: "yeah, but we're not Adidas." You're right. You may only have 100 or 1,000 fans on Facebook, or 100 blog subscribers, or maybe 500 email addresses in your distribution list. But imagine if you partnered with 10 other brands that also target your customers. Let's assume that those brands only have 100, 1,000, or even 10,000 subscribers, fans, or followers. What if you developed a coordinated, content-programming schedule between these brands? Then, you and your partners could reach 1,000, 10,000, or 1 million consumers a day. That's a powerful media brand, and you don't have to bear the burden of creating and distributing all the content alone.

Let me repeat that: You don't have to do it alone. I know you're busy running a business. You don't sell time or space on your website. You're not in the content creation business—and it should stay that way. The solution is to partner with authentic, successful, content creators who your audience already trusts, to create editorially sound content that will drive demand. In other words, you brandscape.

WHAT IF…

In 2010, GEICO spent $745 million on advertising. You know—the ads featuring the talking gecko urging us to save 15 percent by switching insurance companies. What if GEICO spent more on supporting the creation of content than on buying ads?

Let's step back a second and put that kind of advertising buy in perspective. For $745 million, we could actually hire Pixar to write, produce, and animate eight Academy Award-quality feature films like *Finding Nemo*. But *Finding Nemo* isn't going to sell much insurance.

You may already know this (I didn't), but GEICO sells 19 different types of insurance. Even if you divided their ad spend across all 19 lines, each product would still get $39 million to produce content instead of advertising. Let's look at the opportunities to brandscape with this money in just one category: motorcycle insurance.

J&P Cycles is the "world's largest aftermarket parts and accessories superstore." Motorcycle enthusiasts love J&P Cycles. Not only do they sell aftermarket parts for your motorcycle, they have support technicians who will help you install whatever you buy.

J&P Cycles creates tons of content, including "how to" videos designed to help their customers install everything from a luggage rack to a lens grill. On average, they create about 100 videos a year and distribute them freely on YouTube. Their most popular how-to video has been viewed nearly 200,000 times. I know the team at J&P Cycles would love to produce more video for their customers and leads, but that gets expensive and it's time consuming. This is where GEICO fits in.

If GEICO is serious about getting their motorcycle insurance product in front of avid cycle enthusiasts, imagine what J&P Cycles could do with a $39 million video content budget. That's almost a million dollars a week that could go toward video content that's valuable to the audience GEICO is hoping to attract.

What if GEICO invested in every single one of J&P Cycles videos on YouTube? What if GEICO and J&P Cycles worked together to create a compelling half-hour web series for motorcycle riders everywhere? J&P Cycles would serve their customers' needs and GEICO would find their product more relevant, more often, to more people at the right time in their lives.

Brandscaped videos could be distributed to every one of GEICO's motorcycle insurance customers and all of J&P Cycles' existing client base, not to mention the exposure the videos would generate on a platform like YouTube. Both brands would benefit. It's a perfect symbiotic marketing relationship.

Honestly, I don't know what J&P Cycles could, or would, do with a $39 million budget dedicated to content creation, but even if GEICO committed just 10 percent of their motorcycle insurance marketing budget to work with J&P, I guarantee they would both see tremendous results. This would leave GEICO with plenty of extra cash to brandscape with other motorcycle enthusiast brands.

I'll leave you with this: GEICO is owned by Warren Buffett's company, Berkshire Hathaway. At the 2009 Berkshire Hathaway annual meeting, Warren Buffett reportedly indicated that he would spend $2 billion on GEICO ads if he could. What if he spent that money on creating content instead of buying advertising time or space? Imagine the audience he could own. What if J&P Cycles had a $100 million content budget every year?

Ask Yourself...

Who already owns our audience?

In Chapter 1 you began evaluating the products and services your customers buy before they even realize they need your solutions. Now it's time to start evaluating what kind of access those companies have to their audience. Do they have an email database? Do they have a corporate blog, a video channel on YouTube or Vimeo?

Start to consume the content created by these potential brand partners. Maybe their CEO has a blog or participates on Twitter. Sign up for their emails and buy something from their online store so you understand what and how they communicate with their customers.

The more you understand how they engage their audience, the better positioned you'll be to leverage your partnership when the time comes.

Chapter 4
Ignoring One-Hit Wonders

Public Relations?

Public relations has to change. With the media pushing out more and more content, brands can no longer rely on the one-hit-wonder mentality of a traditional public relations campaign. Think about the lifespan of any news story. At best, the impact lasts a week—at worst, a day.

You definitely need a new approach—one that enables you to build a content-based relationship so that if and when the opportunity presents itself to leverage mass-media exposure, you'll be ready. That's exactly what happened with Blendtec.

A Fresh Approach

In 2006, Blendtec, a manufacturer of commercial blenders, was having trouble penetrating the consumer market. They didn't have the mammoth budgets of their competitors—companies that had been around for decades and had spent years advertising in traditional media channels. The marketing team at Blendtec knew they needed a fresh, lower-cost approach.

Blendtec had one major advantage over the competition: they wanted to penetrate a specific market—the blender market. This meant they could hone in on a specific audience. KitchenAid, Oster, and Cuisinart all sell multiple kitchen appliances to a wide range of consumers. Blendtec's ability to focus on buyers in *just* the blender market would prove to be valuable.

As someone who's marketed blenders myself, I can tell you that women make most of the purchase decisions for kitchen appliances, with one important exception—blenders. Young men are often given the task of selecting and purchasing a blender, and they approach the task similar to the way they would purchase a power tool. Blendtec knew this, and they knew they had to attract young males with their marketing strategy.

Exploiting Their Unique Story

Blendtec's blenders have been used in commercial restaurants and smoothie joints for years, and their main selling points have always been durability and power.

Tom Dickson, the CEO and founder of Blendtec, is a hands-on kind of guy. As the inventor behind the Blendtec blender, he tested the product himself. George Wright, Blendtec's vice president of marketing, noticed that Tom's testing methods went way beyond the traditional blender durability and power testing. Tom blended all sorts of weird things to ensure the blades and blender bowl would stand up to the harshest tasks.

"The way he [Tom] tests equipment is very extreme," George says. "He does a lot of crazy things and this blender did a lot of amazing things under this destructive testing."[5]

George realized that Tom's bizarre blender tests would make for great content—content that could speak to the specific needs of their target audience: young males looking for a powerful, durable blender.

Slow Build

George Wright's decision to expose Tom's blender testing techniques to the world seemed like a great idea. A traditional marketer might have created a two-minute corporate video explaining how the rigorous testing results in a high-quality product. Or, perhaps they'd hire a PR firm to get Tom on a talk show to blend some highly unusual items. Instead, George decided to shoot videos of Tom blending bizarre products (things like marbles, credit cards, action figures, and even crowbars) and post them on YouTube. Tom would blend one far-out item per episode, asking a simple question: *Will it Blend?*

George's decision to format the videos more like a challenge than a corporate statement about Blendtec's testing regimen positioned the content as entertainment, rather than marketing. It worked. Within a few days, Blendtec's videos started attracting the attention of YouTube viewers. Within a few months, it had attracted the attention of mass-media outlets, including *Advertising Age* and MSNBC. *Will it Blend?* had become a viral hit.

Newsjack It[6]

After a year of posting semi-monthly videos, the perfect storm of opportunity arrived for Blendtec.

In July 2007, Apple released its first iPhone. People had waited days in line at Apple Stores all around the country for a chance to buy one. So what did Blendtec do when they got their hands on one? They did what they do best—they blended it.

Suddenly, Blendtec had married the day's biggest news event to its product in an authentic way. Thousands of other brands tried to jump on the news bandwagon with videos designed to piggyback on the iPhone story, but *Will it Blend?*—with its year-old audience of loyal viewers and a tried-and-true format—stole the show.

Blendtec was able to leverage the public relations hit in the marketplace (the release of the iPhone) to get more subscribers to their content and ultimately sell more blenders than ever before. More than 100 episodes later, *Will it Blend?* is one of the most subscribed to YouTube channels in history. It has almost 200 million total video views, putting it in the Top 100 YouTube video channels of all time.

Since launching the *Will it Blend?* series, Blendtec's site traffic has increased by 650 percent and sales have increased fivefold. In 2006, Oster enjoyed a brand awareness 43 times that of Blendtec. Today, Blendtec has narrowed that gap to a little less than 1.5—in effect, that's a 2,800 percent increase in brand awareness.

Blendtec doesn't need a PR firm or a PR strategy. Do you?

Access to the Media has been Democratized

Companies spend approximately $8 billion per year on PR services. For decades, PR firms have relied on the strength of their Rolodexes—their media contacts—to help you get in front of the "people who matter." But what if you took all that money and invested it in your own brand, instead of in some PR firm's Rolodex?

Public relations got its start after World War I when a few entrepreneurial war veterans, including a guy named Ivy Lee, decided to take the concepts they'd employed as officers in the U.S.

government's Committee on Public Information and bring them to corporate America.

Ivy Lee described PR as a two-way street. One lane is dedicated to helping companies listen to the public. The other lane communicates corporate messages to the target audience using compelling stories and the media.

I repeat: listen to the public and communicate messages to the target audience using compelling stories and the media. Hmm, that sounds like social media to me.

With the rise of social media, it's never been easier to listen to the public or access the media's content creators in real time. This fundamental shift in the way companies access their two audiences has left many PR professionals stuck in the middle, wondering how to best add value for their clients. In fact, some of the largest PR firms in the world are struggling with the reduced value of their oldest asset, the Rolodex.

In the pre-social media era, access to journalists, reporters, and the media machine in general was extremely limited. You were armed with a fax machine and a phone, or an email account and a website. You were forced to navigate gatekeeper after gatekeeper to try to pitch your brand story to someone who cared.

In the "old days," you could send the writer a press kit via good old-fashioned snail-mail and wait for the phone to ring. Or, you could hire a PR firm that had built trusted, long-term relationships with the media elite you were trying to target. Your PR firm would help craft the right kind of story and then contact the media on your behalf, leveraging that Rolodex of highly valuable media contacts to impact your exposure in the marketplace.

Enter new media channels like Facebook, Twitter, LinkedIn, and even email. As media companies began to publish their writers' email addresses, PR firms (whether they knew it or not) started to lose control of what had become their most valuable asset: the one-to-one, trusted relationship with the media and the journalists behind the scenes.

Essentially, this marked the moment when radio stations, television networks, and print publishers opened media access to the general public (and as a result, corporations) to help create, pitch, and present great stories.

Today, access to the media is easier than ever before. Anyone has a shot at building a trusted relationship with an individual reporter, writer, or even a giant media brand, all but eliminating the need for a PR firm. And not only do you have access to the journalists behind the brand, you have an intimate view of what they're working on at any given time.

Digital Media and the Middle Man

If the digital revolution has done anything, it's helped individuals and companies connect closer and closer to the consumer by bypassing the middlemen. From ecommerce to auctions, digital platforms like Amazon and eBay have enabled entire businesses to flourish by selling directly to the consumer. The PR industry is no different.

In 2008, serial entrepreneur Peter Shankman launched a website called "Help A Reporter Out" (commonly referred to as HARO). This free service "connects news sources with journalists looking for expertise." The premise is simple—any reporter can post a request for a quote, interview, or insight at HelpAReporter.com. As a source, these requests are emailed to you three times a day. All you have to do is find the relevant story requests, reply with your insight, interview information, or expert opinion, and next thing you know you're a source in a bonafide news story.

Everyone from *The New York Times* to *The Huffington Post* uses HARO's free services to add credibility, content, and breadth to their news coverage by uncovering sources they might never have found if it wasn't for the power of Shankman's information marketplace. With more than 30,000 news sources leveraging the platform of 200,000 sources, HARO is a goldmine for brandscapers who understand the value of traditional PR but don't want to pay for the middleman's Rolodex.

I myself have seen the power of HARO. In one week, I responded to one relevant reporter request every day. As a result, I found myself quoted in *The Boston Globe* and on ReadWriteWeb.com and even secured an interview on an Internet radio station. All of this cost me nothing but the time and energy involved in reading and responding to HARO's three emails a day.

HARO is well on its way to helping cut out the PR middleman. If all PR firms continue to provide is access to the media, they won't last. Journalists, reporters, television hosts, celebrities, bloggers, editors, and producers are all online. They're on LinkedIn trolling for stories. They're on Twitter mining hashtags for sources and interviews. They're on Facebook looking for people with a story to tell or an interesting angle and opinion on the things their audience cares about. They're using free services like HARO to get the insight they need when they need it.

Don't get me wrong: there are lots of PR firms that understand that the value of their Rolodex has been completely usurped. Many have expanded their practice to include blogger outreach (a new kind of digital Rolodex of blogs and blogger hubs that influence consumer behavior). However, the firms that are returning to their roots—as great storytellers—are the ones providing clients with the greatest value.

If you're working with a PR partner today, have them focus their energies on helping you connect with journalists, bloggers, and personalities who will add long-term value to your brand. More importantly, enlist their help with crafting compelling stories that position your brand as a source for great information. You can't tell these stories alone. You need your audience, and the media's audience, to embrace your story and elevate it to the point at which it's worth covering.

What's your story? How does your brand add value in the marketplace? Make sure you start connecting with the journalists, bloggers, and influencers in your industry and take Ivy Lee's advice: start listening to what they're covering (in fact, you should already be consuming it). You'll learn a lot in hours, let alone months.

PR is Built for Quick Hits

Public relations as a marketing tactic is something I believe in whole-heartedly. It's something we can leverage to build interest in our brands and the stories we have to tell. However, a good brandscaper knows that great press coverage is the result of a smart strategy and a compelling story told—and re-told—by the right people in a social media-driven world.

Most PR firms are built for creating one-hit wonders. Your brand, product, or thought leaders appear for a brief moment in a modern media landscape that moves so fast the impact is fleeting. For example, *The Huffington Post,* a digital media brand, posted an average of 1,000 news stories per day in 2011.[7] And that's just the volume of one news and opinion source. Multiply that by the tens of thousands of other news and information sources publishing on a daily basis, and it's easy to see how a single-story approach to public relations can't last in a world that moves this fast.

Of course, there is still room for well-crafted, campaign-based PR strategies—but they have to be part of a bigger, long-term content strategy. Blendtec got millions of views for their iPhone episode. This was a very traditional PR success. However, Blendtec already had a semi-monthly series of videos running. It would have been very difficult for them to capitalize on the success of a one-day media explosion had they not already had a loyal audience in place.

Basically, Blendtec was able to translate a one-hit-wonder into a longer-term awareness play. In addition, the huge success garnered by their iPhone episode resulted in an influx of regular subscribers to their web video series on YouTube—something the brand would be able to capitalize on for years to come. This is how modern marketers must start thinking: more about garnering a long-term audience accented and augmented by PR hits.

Mark Lives at Ikea

A few years ago, one of the world's largest public relations firms, Ketchum, put together an award-winning campaign that could have been the start of a long-term content strategy. Instead, their one-hit wonder mentality delivered only short-term results for their client, IKEA. The campaign had all the ingredients for brandscaping success: authentic talent, a great story, and a brand willing to participate.

As you read this story, think of ways that IKEA and Ketchum could have turned this single-story sensation into a longer-term strategy.

In 2008, Mark Malkoff was already something of a YouTube personality. As a comedian and filmmaker living in New York City, he had made quite a name for himself playing the naked cowboy in Times Square, and he'd proven his success as a stuntman of sorts by visiting all 177 Starbucks in Manhattan in 24 hours.

As the story goes, Mark came home one day to find himself in quite a predicament. His tiny apartment was getting fumigated and he needed to find a place to stay for a whole week in less than 24 hours. None of his friends could help him out, and hotels were too expensive. Mark had no idea where to go.

As he looked around his apartment, Mark realized that 80 percent of his furnishings came from IKEA. That's when he had an epiphany. IKEA would be the perfect place to stay while his apartment was being fumigated. IKEA has 24-hour security. It's fully furnished. It even offers complimentary food service and has thousands of square feet of living space. Spending a week at IKEA would be wonderful!

Mark asked IKEA if he could stay in the Paramus, New Jersey, store in exchange for creating a series of online video shows. IKEA, with the guidance of its public relations firm Ketchum, agreed.

Over the next week, Mark spent 24 hours a day in the expansive IKEA just across the river from Manhattan. He videotaped, edited, and uploaded at least one video a day. He had 24-hour access to interview IKEA customers and staff, and to roam the entire store. The videos he uploaded were fun and he was having a great time, but the separation from his wife starting taking a toll. So Mark invited singer/songwriter Lisa Loeb to serenade his frustrated wife. Lisa agreed, and in exchange for an IKEA desk set, she performed a concert right in the middle of the IKEA store, much to the delight of the bewildered and starstruck customers and staff.

Mark uploaded 25 videos that generated more than 1.5 million video views that week. The website he set up, MarkLivesAtIkea.com, attracted 15 million visitors and the quirky concept generated a huge amount of media attention. Mark appeared on everything from the *Today Show* to local radio stations around the country. The total tally by the end of the week, according to Ketchum, came in at 382 million positive brand impressions on a budget that totaled $13,500.

A week after it all started, it was over. Mark went home and Ketchum and IKEA moved on. It didn't matter that IKEA claimed this campaign was the most successful in its U.S. history. It didn't matter that the store's sales rose by 5.5 percent and its website traffic increased by 6.8 percent. Mark, IKEA, and Ketchum parted ways.

Stop Manufacturing Stories

One of the reasons the IKEA campaign was so successful was because the story wasn't manufactured. It was 100 percent authentic.

Mark really *did* need to find a place to stay. Mark really *does* own a lot of IKEA furniture. Mark really *is* a good comedian and a skillful storyteller and filmmaker. I don't think a room full of professional PR people could've ever manufactured a more effective campaign than the one born out of Mark's authentic love for IKEA.

If you've been guilty of manufacturing stories in the past, start looking for authentic ones stemming from the real-life experiences, needs, and desires of your existing customers. Get to know the individuals who are already writing about, talking about, and participating in the online communities you serve. Package those stories and the personalities behind them and start delivering them to your audience on a regular basis. Look at your efforts as part of a long-term strategy. It is completely unrealistic in this day-and-age to think that a few media surges are going to create long-term demand for your products or services. Start thinking more like Blendtec and less like IKEA. Say goodbye to the one-hit wonder.

WHAT IF...

Instead of ending the campaign, what if IKEA would have capitalized on the audience the *Mark Lives at IKEA* show built? What if they would have continued their relationship with Mark? He already proved he could attract an audience. He'd shown that he was capable of booking celebrity guests like Lisa Loeb. What if Mark Malkoff was the next Conan O'Brien or Jay Leno? What if IKEA thought more like Blendtec?

What if Mark Malkoff hosted a daily comedy show right from the IKEA showroom floor? Mark could have his choice of sets ranging from kitchens for cooking segments to living rooms for interviews. Every guest who appeared on the show could go home happy with one piece of IKEA furniture, just like Lisa Loeb.

Think a live streaming web show can't possibly work? Meet a self-proclaimed geek rocker named Matthew Ebel. Every week since 2007, Matthew Ebel has been broadcasting a live show from his basement on Tuesday nights. Matthew's show isn't over-produced. It's authentically shot in his basement, which he lovingly calls The Coffee Bunker. Armed with a keyboard, a webcam, and a microphone, Matthew interacts with his audience, takes song requests and plays an intimate concert for interested fans.

Matthew's music isn't for everyone. It's targeted specifically at geeks and his weekly show has attracted them en masse. With half a million views over five years, each episode attracts an average of 2,500 fans from around the world. His live concerts connect with his fan base in an intimate way that has built his music career. His loyal fan base has funded a world tour and they even buy subscriptions to his music with one new song released every two weeks. Matthew Ebel is an authentic content creator with a live weekly show that attracts a loyal and valuable audience.

What if Matthew Ebel became Mark Malkoff's house-band, live from IKEA? Matthew could be the Paul Schaeffer to Mark's David Letterman. What if Mark and Matt's audience joined forces? Geeks around the world would immediately tune-in to watch.

IKEA's show could be streamed live to the web using a channel like

Ustream or Livestream. The producers could even leverage these technologies to link up with other IKEA stores around the nation to feature remote guests or musical acts.

The truth is, I don't know why IKEA and Mark didn't keep it going. I can only speculate it wasn't for budgetary reasons (the first week's worth of episodes only cost about 3.5 cents per 1,000 impressions). I can also assume it wasn't because IKEA felt the campaign was a flop, considering that sales actually increased. This leads me to believe they were thinking like traditional marketers and PR people—they were more focused on their one-hit wonder than on the opportunity to create long-term, sustainable growth and audience development.

What if IKEA had turned Mark's one-hit wonder into an ever-growing digital success?

Ask Yourself...

What can we learn from our previous PR hits to prepare for the next one?

Your previous one-hit wonders shouldn't be disregarded as lucky PR placements. Sort through all your old mentions (no matter how old) and start looking for trends. What kinds of stories generate interest in your brand? Start thinking about ways you can start creating content today that can grow an audience interested in those kinds of stories over the long term. Who else is mentioned, referenced, or included in those stories? What kind of content are they creating? Who are they creating it with? Leave no angle unturned. Leverage your next PR success to drive audience growth *and* sales, just like Blendtec did.

Chapter 5
Death to the Inauthentic Celebrity

So Long, Phony Spokesperson

The idea of attaching talent to your brand isn't new. Companies have been using celebrities to hawk their products for years. But do you really believe that George Foreman grills up low-fat meals on the George Foreman Grill? Or that O.J. Simpson used to rent cars from Hertz?

In the advertising industry, it's common practice to hire a famous spokesperson to help raise awareness for products and services. But this gimmicky practice isn't limited to advertising. For decades, PR firms have secured promotional relationships with celebrities in order to "authentically" attach the celebrity's persona to the brands the PR firm represents.

But in today's social media landscape—where celebrities tweet their every move, update their status on Facebook, and upload home movies to YouTube—hiring a spokesperson who doesn't actually use your products or subscribe services is not a good investment. Just think—if George Foreman went out to dinner every night and checked into every restaurant he visited on Foursquare (but never actually cooked at home on the grill that bears his name) would the grill manufacturer benefit from the audience George is building on social media? Obviously not.

In a digital world where trust-based relationships, honest insight, and genuine brand affinities exist, the traditional notion of hiring a celebrity spokesperson has changed. Success in social media thrives on authenticity. If the audience thinks a celebrity is getting paid to endorse something he or she doesn't actually use or believe in, the audience won't believe in it either.

Really, Chelsea?

Your audience of fans, followers, and friends is smarter than you give them credit for.

It was no secret that Chelsea Handler, comedienne, talk show host, and author of four *New York Times* best sellers including *Are You There, Vodka? It's Me Chelsea,* drank Grey Goose vodka. Yet suddenly, as she embarked on a nationwide book tour to promote her third book, *Chelsea Chelsea Bang Bang,* she switched to Belvedere. When asked why in an interview with *Ad Age,* Chelsea said, "I was a Grey Goose girl but I found out Belvedere has no real sugar in it...these guys really know what they're talking about. They have a distillery in Poland and that spells serious to me. Plus, if I was going to have someone sponsor me, it would have to be either Belvedere or Kotex. I just like Belvedere better."

I'm no vodka connoisseur, but that sounds like an inauthentic marketing pitch manufactured in a public relations training session Chelsea had just before the *Ad Age* interview. The truth is, Belvedere vodka decided to pony up a lot of cash to sponsor her book tour, and Grey Goose didn't.

If I can't trust Chelsea when she tells me she loves Grey Goose, no wait, Belvedere, what can I trust? In 2011, she tweeted to her 4.5 million fans that *Wanderlust* was the "funniest movie" she'd seen all year. "It comes out Friday and if you want to pee in your pants, go see it," she wrote. But how can I be sure she's not just trying to pump up her ratings (the movie's star, Jennifer Aniston, was that night's guest on Chelsea's television show), or maybe *Wanderlust's* producers were paying her to say that?

In an authentic social media world, it's better to retain your audience's trust by forming authentic, long-term brand relationships that are true to both the brand sponsor and the talent, than it is to flip-flop around to whomever's willing to pay the highest dollar to be attached to a personality. Trust me, your audience sees right through it, and it affects everything you say on every channel you participate in. Most importantly, an inauthentic brand relationship does nothing to win you new, loyal customers.

Authentic Talent is Everywhere

Today, anyone can become a digital celebrity. With a smartphone and a YouTube channel, you can start creating video content. With a computer and an Internet connection, you can start a blog for free. With a digital camera, you can start uploading photos to Flickr. You can open a Twitter account or join Google+. On every one of these channels, you can create quality content and build a valuable audience. If you do it well enough, you can become just as influential as Ashton Kutcher, Chelsea Handler, or Will Ferrell.

For every author who authentically likes Grey Goose, there's one who loves Belvedere. There's no reason to create false "sponsored" relationships. The rise of the digital celebrity makes a celebrity endorsement accessible to every brand selling any product or service. Why manufacture a false relationship when your real customers want to be part of your universe?

No matter how big or small your company is, I guarantee you can find the right content creator who really does love what you make (or what you do) who can create content to draw others to your brand. You can also find talented people already creating content on their own YouTube channels or blogs who have the potential to increase demand for your products or services. These new media personalities have their own built-in audiences and many of them would love to have your marketing support to gain greater visibility. That visibility, in turn, has the potential to increase your sales overnight.

But you don't have to stop there—you can even turn your own company's thought leaders and executives into branded personalities, just like Blendtec did with its CEO Tom Dickson. Channels like YouTube, Flickr, Twitter, and even your blog, make doing so easier than ever.

Anyone who's seen the feature film *Julie & Julia* understands the potential power of creating content in the new media world. The movie is based on a memoir by Julie Powell, a call-center attendant who embarked on a quest to bring meaning to her life by attempting to cook every recipe in Julia Child's book, *Mastering the Art of French Cooking*. Everyday, Julie, who also happens to be a talented writer, chronicled her quest in the form of blog posts (http://juliepowell. blogspot.com/).

Julie started the project in 2002 and before she'd even completed all 524 recipes in the cook book, she had her own book deal with a traditional publisher. Her book, *Julie and Julia: 365 Days, 524 Recipes, 1 Tiny Apartment Kitchen*, became a *New York Times* best seller and, later, a successful feature film. Nora Ephron wrote the screenplay, and Meryl Streep was nominated for an Oscar for her performance as Julia Child.

Imagine if you were Williams-Sonoma, the high-end kitchen retail chain, and you'd been looking for great content that inspires people to cook at home more often? Imagine if you'd discovered Julie Powell? Julie's book was so successful in reigniting a movement for traditional French cooking, that *Mastering the Art of French Cooking* topped the *New York Times* best seller list for the first time in its 40-year history.

Talent agents and scouts are really good at finding and picking up new talent as soon as people are interested in buying their content (or companies express interest in paying them as a spokesperson), and that's been their business model for decades. However, with the amount of content being created in very narrow niches ranging from graphic design for PowerPoint presentations, to local restaurant reviews, to best techniques for electrical soldering, no talent scout can find your next celebrity hit. It would take an army of agents to uncover the deep opportunities in any one specific market.

So, as you are watching and listening to the influencers creating content in your niche, start thinking more like a talent agent. Try to align yourself with the next big thing in your industry. If you find these people early enough, you can be a big part of their success. Ask them about their dreams and ambitions. Work to build a symbiotic relationship that can improve your sales or even prompt you to expand your offerings. Wouldn't you rather form these types of genuine partnerships than pay for some phony endorsement? Don't you think your audience would thank you for it?

WHAT IF...

What if Russell Hobbs, Inc., the company that manufactures the George Foreman Grill, reinvigorated their brand and grill sales by partnering with a completely authentic content creator instead of a former heavyweight champion?

It's rumored that George Foreman made more than $200 million from his endorsement of the countertop grill that bears his name. Sure, the infomercials he starred in helped make the grill a household staple and the content in those commercials is extremely enticing, but it's been almost two decades since the first ads aired. Where does that leave the grill today?

It turns out the George Foreman Grill has been embraced by an entire generation of college coeds. In fact, CheapScholar.org, a website dedicated to helping make college affordable, recommended that college students invest in a 'Foreman Grill and cut back on their university meal plan to save on college tuition. But CheapScholar isn't the only content creator targeting college-age kids with content about the value of the George Foreman Grill.

Take Big Girls, Small Kitchen, for example. They've created an entire website dedicated to college cooking called Small Kitchen College (college.biggirlssmallkitchen.com). The blog's 44 contributors are dorm-room chefs who make the most out of cooking healthy, fun, and delicious meals without a full kitchen.

One of their contributors, Sarah Leibach, describes herself as a senior at The George Washington University with a "…somewhat unhealthy crush on her [George Foreman] Grill."[8] Already, that sounds like a ringing (and incredibly authentic) endorsement for the brand. But it doesn't end there.

Sarah wrote a wonderful article titled, "Look Ma, No Oven! Grilling with George Foreman." In the piece, Sarah goes on to outline exactly why it's the perfect college dorm appliance.

"Like the dorm micro-fridge or the spork, a George Foreman Grill is one of those genius all-in-one inventions that you don't know you need until it solves all of your problems," Sarah espouses. "…These babies can act as an oven, stovetop, or toaster in one simple device. Best of all, they come in all sizes (and prices) to accommodate your life," she adds.

Sarah then goes on to reveal her three favorite 'Foreman Grill recipes: Foreman Fajitas, Sliders and Sweet Potato Fries, and Big Kid Grilled Cheese. She even includes an appetizing and beautifully shot picture of her sumptuous sliders.

Sarah isn't the only contributor on Big Girls, Small Kitchen that's featured ideas for expanding your mind using the 'Foreman Grill. At least two other contributors seem to have the same affinity for the dorm-room appliance.

What if Russell Hobbs, Inc., got behind the idea that college dorm-room cooking can be a reality with only one appliance? What if the marketing whiz's behind the 'Foreman Grill offered to create a Big Girls, Small Kitchen version of the grill and leveraged Sarah's weekly content to inspire college kids to embrace the simple cooking ideas she adores?

What if Russell Hobbs invested even one percent of what they paid George Foreman to create a college-dorm cookbook and paid to syndicate that content on college campus websites as a weekly feature? With $2 million, Sarah—along with Big Girls, Small Kitchen—could begin building a movement to get college kids to start cooking.

Every year, 20 million students are enrolled in colleges and universities in America. Imagine if Sarah and her team managed to convince five percent of those students to purchase a $20 'Foreman Grill every year? Russell Hobbs would see a 1,000 percent return on investment in the first year!

These types of organic, authentic relationships with consumers who already embrace your brand need scale, strategy, and resources. But very often they reveal opportunities to tap a market you might never have considered before you took the time to understand where your brand drives value in the marketplace.

What if every dorm room in America got cooking with Sarah and her favorite grill?

Ask Yourself...

Who has already authentically embraced our brand?

No matter how small their audience, it's time you started keeping track of all the bloggers, YouTubers, Instagrammers, podcasters, and Tweeters who authentically embrace your brand. Create a list so you can refer back to it often.

You need to not only consume the content they create, but also rank the content they consume and start learning more about their audience. The more you discover about the talent that powers your brand, the more you'll start seeing the opportunities to engage these content creators in more meaningful ways.

Start looking for content "gems"—the rough ideas that, with a little spit and polish, could really become entertaining and engaging. Look for the "X-factor," that unexplainable "something" that charismatic content creators possess.

Start thinking of yourself as a brand talent scout and embrace those who've already embraced you.

Chapter 6
The Insatiable Demand for Content

You Need Content, Not Tactics

I know—you're on Facebook, your company's tweeting, you started a Tumblog (on Tumblr), you're pinning crap on Pinterest, you uploaded a video to YouTube, your Flickr feed is neglected, and your SlideShare account lies dormant. Meanwhile, you've got a website that needs updating, a blog you post on as often as possible, and an email newsletter you think could be better. You're running ads in a trade magazine, your Yelp reviews keep coming in, you just met with your PR firm, and you're trying to measure the impact of all of this. Every channel, every platform, each agency, and every media outlet you participate with demands more time, more energy, more money, and more content.

If there's one thing the proliferation of digital media has created, it's an insatiable demand for content from your customers, your friends, your followers, your fans, your subscribers, your leads, and your partners. You need status updates and images, PowerPoint presentations and podcasts, videos, and infographics. You still need ads and press releases, trade show signs, and direct-mail pieces. You need tweets and LinkedIn answers, not to mention something for the webinar you're hosting this week.

You don't need a bunch of social media tactic tutorials or a day-long session on how to use LinkedIn. You need a new strategy to focus your energies and efforts on driving more revenue. Today, your marketing team creates more and measures less. That's got to change, and it all starts by realizing that you have to make an appointment with your audience. You have to get them to start consuming your content on a regularly scheduled basis.

Information Overload

Just because you're developing more content doesn't mean your audience is consuming it. The amount of information created in the always-on digital world streams by at an unbelievable pace. Let's go back half a century to look at the content consumption habits of the average consumer.

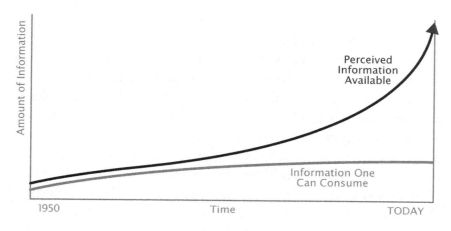

INFORMATION OVERLOAD

Figure 1: Consumers have access to more information—but that doesn't mean they can consume all the information available.

Figure 1 represents the gap between the information one can consume and the perception of the information available. As you can see, the amount of information accessible by consumers has skyrocketed since 1990. That's because anyone can be a publisher these days, and marketers, news organizations, magazines, television networks and bloggers are all creating more and more content.

Just because consumers have more access to information now than they did in the pre-Internet days doesn't mean they can consume 10, 20, or 30 times more content than they used to. Can they consume more than they did 50 or 60 years ago? Sure, but they certainly can't consume all of it.

In a world where your consumers are bombarded with information from every brand on the planet—not to mention news organizations, family blogs, photo-sharing sites, viral video spam, and, of course,

Nigerian royalty sending out offers of riches beyond belief—how do you move from being part of the problem to being part of the solution? You find the most effective channels for reaching your own particular audience and then you get them to consume your content on a regularly scheduled basis. You build a relationship, through your content, with the customers you're looking to attract.

The Joe Show

The Advertising Specialty Institute (ASI) has found a way to cut through the clutter of information overload with a weekly video program on YouTube called *The Joe Show*. Those of you in the promotional products business probably already know Joe. For those of you who don't, here's a quick primer.

You know those logo pens, party glow sticks, t-shirts, thumb drives, and logo-ladened coffee mugs you get at trade shows? Those are called promotional products. If you've ever seen a promotional products catalog, you know that the options and ideas are endless. The promotional products business is an $18 billion industry and ASI is its trade association. ASI publishes a magazine and hosts industry events, but in 2008 it also began producing *The Joe Show*.

Imagine if your job was to sell promotional products every single day. It's a tough job. You would need some motivation. You would need some inspiration. That's where *The Joe Show* comes in. Each week, without fail, Joe Haley, one of the editors from ASI's trade publication, hosts a three- to four-minute video that showcases new promotional products you could suggest to your clients. Sure, the product ideas are timely and relevant. But more importantly, Joe enthusiastically delivers ideas on how to sell these products to your clients. Joe is fun, genuine, easily excitable, and a real personality. He's a promotional products celebrity. Whether he's showcasing a flashing LED-sequined hat, inflatable clappers, or logo-emblazoned plastic cups, Joe helps fire-up promotional sales staff to pick up the phones and start making calls! (Wanna watch an episode? http://bit.ly/thejoeshow)

Joe understands his audience. He knows what they need: motivation to make another call with a new promotional idea to talk about. He's formatted his show to deliver relevant information every week and he's built a loyal following. Joe doesn't expect or need to have millions of YouTube viewers. He has about 1,000 YouTube subscribers and attracts around 500 viewers a week. For those 500 weekly video viewers, Joe is an invaluable resource. His shows increase demand for every product showcased.

Take it from Joe—you don't need a "viral success." You need a high-quality audience that subscribes to your content and looks forward to receiving it on a predictable basis.

Stop Chasing the Social Stream

Everyone—from your local newspaper and TV stations to your competition in the marketplace—is creating more content in the hopes that your audience will consume it. This is the perceived opportunity: create more crap and my audience will consume more. But the truth is, consumers are actually ignoring more content than ever. This is the paradox of information overload.

If you want to create content that fits into the consumption habits and routines of your audience, you have to stop measuring your success by the *quantity* of consumption, and start creating content that builds long-term relationships with *higher-quality* consumers. The way to deal with your audience's information overload head-on is to frequently deliver high-quality content that's *relevant* to them.

The most successful brands are not creating more content, they're creating *better* content that solidifies relationships and drives demand for their products and services. They're creating content their audience *wants* to consume on a regular basis.

So stop chasing the social stream of content that's flying by at millions of posts per second, and start creating content your audience actually wants to consume.

In a digital world, where it's so easy to create more content, more often, we must resist the urge to pursue the idea that more content means more results. Good brandscapers focus on creating higher-quality content designed to generate higher-quality leads or more loyal customers. They combat the paradox of information overload by building relationships with their audiences that add value to their lives through content. They make their customers look smarter and live better by becoming part of their content consumption habits and routines.

If you stopped sending your email newsletter out each month, day, or week, would anyone notice? If not, you are contributing to information overload.

WHAT IF...

One of the ways marketers, consultants, brands, and experts are trying to combat the phenomenon of information overload is by curating valuable content for their targeted audience. Essentially, they're sifting through all the relevant content created on the web and contextualizing, even ranking, it on one website to help their audience consume the most valuable information in a more efficient and effective manner.

Suites of tools and even new companies have sprung up to help brands and content publishers manage, suggest, review, and re-post content around niches ranging from environmentally friendly data warehousing and cell-phone towers to NASCAR drivers and travel destinations. But no tool can do what Dave Pell has done.

Dave Pell is a self-proclaimed "curation savant" and "Internet superhero." He's a technology entrepreneur and well-respected writer. But what's most interesting about Dave is how often his email newsletter is opened and consumed.

Dave's daily email, NextDraft, is sent to 10,000 opt-in subscribers. More than 65 percent of his audience opens and consumes his curated content.[9] (To put Dave's numbers in perspective, the average email newsletter open rate in Q1 2012 was 26.2 percent.)[10] So what kind of content could be so compelling that his audience consumes it each and every day? Dave's links to "The Day's Most Fascinating News."

Each day, Dave spends around three hours scouring 50 or 60 websites looking for the stories he thinks are the most interesting or important. He hones that list to about 10 links, expounds on each story with some witty commentary, and hits the send button. His stories aren't the ones you'll see in *The New York Times* or hear about on CNN—they're the stories that, in an information-laden world, can rapidly fly under the radar.

"Everybody's so overwhelmed by the incoming tweets and Facebook status updates and never-ending news cycle that they need some way to sift through it and find the good stuff they *should* be paying attention to," Dave said in a recent interview on PandoDaily.com.[11] Dave's used his ability to filter through that information to build a loyal and valuable audience.

Dave has actually built some of his own curation assistant tools, like Addictomatic.com, to help him on his quest to find the best stuff. Go ahead, sign up for his newsletter. You, too, will find yourself embracing "the day's most fascinating news."

So what's Dave's perspective on cutting through information overload? "We're getting to the point with the amount of information that people are being asked to absorb that it almost feels more like a responsibility or an anvil or a weight that's attached to us. To the extent that someone can say, 'Let me take that weight off you. I'll do the heavy lifting. You can just go about your daily life, and once a day I'll send you a list of stuff you might be interested in.' I think there's a benefit to that." You should, too.

What if you bought into the simple idea that curating the most valuable content from other sources, even your competitors, and sharing it with your leads or prospects increases their trust in your brand and the likelihood they'll engage with your company?

What if you leveraged a content curation tool to find the most under-consumed, but highest-value content for your audience? What if you contextualized and then emailed that content to your leads? What if you introduced your prospects to content that impacts their business—content that cuts through the clutter of information instead of adding to it? What if you followed Dave Pell's lead and worked to combat information overload?

Ask Yourself...

What can we stop doing now to afford ourselves the opportunity to create something of higher value?

Go ahead: Make a list of all the marketing-oriented activities you do on a monthly basis. List everything. Include the white papers and the promotional emails. Don't forget the webinars (and all the things that you do to promote them). What about the tweets, the blog posts, the status updates, and the giveaways?

I know you're resource-strapped, but one of the problems we all face is making the hard decisions to stop doing things that don't add enough value. You really need to stop doing the things that add to information overload. Sure, some people open your emails and some of them actually sign up for your webinars. But to be an effective brandscaper you have to realize that anything you attempt is going to be more effective if you stop doing the things that aren't.

You need to shift your focus to providing higher-value content with a predictable frequency to build a valuable audience. So stop doing too many half-assed things and put those resources to work doing one thing better than anyone else on the web.

What can you stop doing today so you can start doing something better tomorrow?

Chapter 7
We Live in an Opt-in World

A Subscription is a Commitment

A subscription to content has always been one of the most basic commitments a consumer can make to a brand or media entity. It's the start of a relationship based on the generation and distribution of high-quality, relevant, frequently delivered content.

Magazines, newspapers, cable TV companies, and catalogers used to own the word "subscribe." However, that all began to change with the rise of email marketing, when brands and companies started inviting their customers to "subscribe" to their monthly email newsletters or weekly deals.

Think about all the content you can subscribe to today. You can subscribe to a YouTube channel, a Facebook fan page (with the Like button), or a tweet stream. You can subscribe to an RSS feed from a blog, or even a set of Google search results and alerts. I subscribe to podcasts, Netflix video streaming, mobile app updates, and text message alerts for everything from my airline updates to the local newspaper.

We live in a world of constantly flowing subscriptions to content. I know people who subscribe to group discount websites and coupon alerts. I'm sure you subscribe to an industry newsletter, or perhaps an industry data source. Maybe you also subscribe to company updates and career change notices on LinkedIn, or group alerts that keep you informed about the discussions taking place in your favorite forums.

The words "follow," "like," "fan," and "connect" are all today's synonyms for the very simple concept of subscribing. But what exactly is a consumer "subscribing" to when he or she makes a commitment to your brand? Every person who "follows" your company on Twitter is expecting valuable insight, information, content, or maybe coupons to be delivered on a frequent basis from your brand. The same goes for other brands in the marketplace.

Media companies no longer own the word subscribe. We all do. But have you thought about what that means to your company, employees, and clients? It means you have an obligation.

Setting Expectations

When you subscribe to a magazine, newspaper, or a cable network you know what to expect. If you tune-in to CNBC on a regular basis, you don't expect your programming to include music videos. If you listen to NPR, you don't expect Top 40 radio. When people subscribe to your content, it doesn't mean they're interested in everything you put out. It means they're interested in a specific subset of your insight and information.

Even with a channel as simple as Twitter, it's important to understand why your audience should, would, could, or does subscribe to your content. Are they opting-in to a long line of promotional discounts? Do you plan on mixing your personal experiences with valuable industry insight? Are you tweeting the Soup of the Day? The more focused your content strategy is on any opt-in platform, the more successful you'll be. You'll garner a larger audience, find yourself shared more often, and ultimately, be more effective in gaining the trust of your audience, customers, and clients. It's also important to set this expectation up early—before someone subscribes to your content. After that, it's up to you to meet their expectations.

Tom O'Keefe has built himself a little Twitter empire with his handle @BostonTweet. Even before you decide to subscribe to his tweet stream, Tom tells you exactly what you can expect in his Twitter bio: "BostonTweet is all about life in Boston, things to do of value in the city, food and drink deals, news, pics, burritos, and where I am." Even a quick look at his content reveals a deep commitment to his audience. "Does late-night food get any better than Bolognese macaroni for $5 at Eastern Standard?" Or, "Tonight @BrewerySession No. 3 is featuring Somerville's @SlumBrew on tap, paired with live local music at Atwood's."

Tom's been tweeting stuff at an average of 12 tweets a day since 2008 and he's built up a loyal following of college students, foodies, and even Boston visitors. Tom's digital success and focus has even translated into off-line attention. He's been featured on local TV stations and newspapers and he's often recognized on public transportation (an average of six times a day).

Tom doesn't devalue his tweet stream with links to irrelevant content. He doesn't distract his audience with political opinions or sports updates. You can go elsewhere for that. Tom continuously grows his audience by delivering on his promise to add value to your life in Boston.

Tom's audience is not only large (he reaches around 10 percent of the Boston population), it's also powerful. With an audience that valuable, he's actually been able to monetize his passion by building a brandscape.

Brandscaping Your Audience

Partnering with others who find your opt-in audience of value is one of the key tenants to creating a successful brandscaping strategy. Tom's focused content has been designed to meet his audience's expectations. And his success has been rewarded in a unique partnership between BostonTweet and Groupon, without compromising the quality of his content.

Groupon, a website that provides its subscribers with daily deals on fun local things to do, has used Tom's digital success to help small businesses understand the value of digital media. In essence, Tom receives a monthly retainer to consult with some of the restaurants, bars, and local jaunts that need digital support—courtesy of Groupon. Four years after Tom started tweeting, he's driving a six-figure income.

Tom understands the commitment he's made to his opt-in audience and does nothing to jeopardize his credibility. Even as he consults with small businesses, he maintains the credibility of this tweet stream by ensuring that he's not mixing paid clients (on Groupon's platform) with his valuable and trusted recommendations. In fact, his tweets are so valuable that the *Travel Channel* has syndicated his tweet stream. Tom is one small step closer to his dream of hosting a *Travel Channel* television show and it all started with 140-character strategy—a strategy that's built a valuable, opt-in audience fed and fueled by a steady stream of 15 tweets a day.

Extremely Targeted Content

Take a minute to explore Dell's Twitter strategy. Instead of creating one Twitter handle for all things Dell, the company has more than 30 different tweet streams. @DellOutlet tweets discounts and deals on refurbished computers, @DellEDU helps educators leverage technology in their classrooms, and @DellHealth strives to be "your source for health IT news/updates."

Dell understands the need to develop content specifically for the audiences it's targeting. It's highly unlikely that the 1.5 million @DellOutlet followers are all interested in the @DellEDU content. Meanwhile, the 30,000 followers interested in leveraging technology for their classrooms aren't inundated with discount codes for refurbished laptops. And it works. Since 2007, Dell's driven an average of $1 million per year in revenue from the @DellOutlet tweet stream for one simple reason: they understand the power of the word "subscribe" and the audience's expectations for their content.

Whether you're a one-man show, like @BostonTweet, or a large corporation like Dell, setting an expectation for the kind of content you're going to deliver and then consistently fulfilling that promise will unlock the key to your audience's purchasing power. A good brandscaper treats every "like," "fan," "follow," or "subscribe" with the understanding that their audience has made a commitment to their content. Are you meeting your audience's expectations?

WHAT IF...

Accenture is the world's largest consulting company. It's a Fortune 500 company that services companies of all kinds, ranging from financial services to media and communications. One of their vertical practices serves the insurance industry.

Accenture has a YouTube channel and over the course of three years has uploaded 193 videos. That's an average of one per week. Unfortunately, for the 1,200 people who've subscribed to Accenture's channel, there's no expectation of what or when they'll deliver some new insight to their audience.

One of the Accenture shows, *Insurance Chart of the Week*, specifically targets the insurance industry. Given the name of the show, I'd expect to receive some new insight and an industry-relevant chart once a week on YouTube. Unfortunately, Accenture doesn't fulfill that commitment. Over 18 months, they only uploaded 21 videos in the series. (That doesn't add up to one each week.)

Let's assume for a moment that I subscribed to the Accenture YouTube channel with the expectation I'd receive my insurance chart and insight every week. I would have been disappointed. I made a commitment to their content and they didn't keep up their end of the bargain.

What if Accenture created an Accenture Insurance YouTube channel? What if they set and then met their commitment to deliver insurance insight on a regular, predictable basis? Over the course of a year, insurance professionals would have gained knowledge and built trust with Accenture's consulting professionals.

What if *you* set and maintain your audience's expectations for your content? What if you took the time to leverage the power of a content subscription?

Ask Yourself...
What expectations have we set for our audience?

Every company I know has an email database (even if it's just an Excel spreadsheet). But few, if any, have set expectations for the information and insight they've committed to deliver to a committed audience.

Dave Pell (the guy behind NextDraft) has a very simple email newsletter sign-up page. (Check it out at http://bit.ly/nextdraft.) He sets your expectations with one line: "The day's most fascinating news." So does SAY Media (a digital content provider). Their email sign-up says, "Friday is Venn-day. Get it every week." Yep, you guessed it, every week they send me a new Venn diagram and an accompanying article. I've come to expect and enjoy them.

If you're not setting and meeting the expectations for the audience you have, you don't have an audience. It's just a list of email addresses. So take some time to figure out what you're going to send your audience and when you're going to send it. Start with one piece of valuable content on a regular basis and immediately you'll begin building a relationship with your email list. It's the only way to turn a list into an ownable asset.

Chapter 8
You're Not the Center of the Web World

Getting Over Your Website

Your website is not the center of anyone's universe. Channels such as Facebook, Twitter, YouTube, Amazon, and Google are digital destinations unlike anything you could ever imagine building.

You can spend tons of money on digital ads or even television commercials trying to convince people to come to your website, and maybe they will. They might come once, maybe even twice. But they're visiting YouTube, Facebook, and their favorite blogs and news websites every day.

It's time you start focusing on the many opportunities outside of your domain. Done right, it's possible to take a company from almost no revenue to $10 million in annual revenue in less than two years. Just ask Orabrush.

Do You Have Bad Breath?

For more than a decade, Dr. Bob Wagstaff tried to sell his invention—a tongue cleaner called Orabrush. He had taken the toothbrush for your tongue to Oral-B and every major retailer, but no one wanted to carry his product. He even hired a direct-to-consumer marketing firm and spent $50,000 creating an infomercial, which resulted in the sale of about 100 brushes.

As a last-ditch effort, he invited a room full of MBA students from Brigham Young University to help him examine the viability of the product. The students determined that 92 percent of the retail market wasn't interested in a tongue cleaner. As Dr. Bob took in the disappointing news, one student named Jeffrey Harmon raised his hand and asked Dr. Bob what he thought about targeting the eight percent of people who *did* want a tongue brush. In a market like the United States with 300 million consumers, Jeffrey thought that if he could reach the 24 million consumers who wanted a tongue cleaner, Dr. Bob could be successful.

Jeffrey also thought they'd have a better chance selling the product online. He believed that if their messaging got closer to the target market's everyday online experience, they could sell Dr. Bob's Orabrush. Dr. Bob liked what he heard, and he and Jeff teamed up to give it a shot.

Working nights and weekends, Jeffrey experimented with his theory. He found a generic video about how to tell if you have bad breath on YouTube and posted it to his Facebook page. Immediately, he saw his conversion rate triple. People who *knew* they had bad breath needed an Orabrush.

Suddenly, Jeffrey saw that if he could help people realize they have bad breath, he could actually increase demand for the product. So, for $500, Jeffrey and his brother Neal teamed up to create a fun and entertaining video starring a friend of theirs, Austin Craig, that succinctly explained how to tell if you have bad breath. It's simple really. Scrape your tongue gingerly with a spoon and let the spoon dry. Now, smell the spoon. If it smells bad, you've got bad breath. (Go ahead, try it.)

With a $40 YouTube ad, Jeffrey began seeing results. The video attracted 13 to 17-year-old males and females, a demographic eager to ensure their breath isn't a distraction. Jeffrey knew that it was highly likely that this was the eight percent of people who were actually interested in buying a tongue brush.

In the five weeks following the YouTube launch, Orabrush sold 10,000 units. Dr. Bob ordered more and he sold out again. Jeffrey's approach had worked. Inquiries poured in from more than 40 countries, asking if they could distribute the Orabrush. Still, Walmart and the domestic retailers weren't interested, even though tens of thousands of YouTube viewers had asked in the comments section of the videos why they couldn't go down to the local store and buy an Orabrush.

Meanwhile, one of the local Walmart managers in Utah, where Orabrush is based, had seen the video, ordered a brush, and liked the product. He decided to carry it. Sales were so good that after a local store tour by other Utah-based Walmart managers, 20 additional Walmart stores decided to carry the brush.

But Orabrush wanted to go national and they wouldn't take no for an answer. The team created and sent a personalized DVD to the head buyer at Walmart—but still, nothing. So Jeffery bought a $28 Facebook ad specifically targeted to Walmart employees in and around the corporate headquarters. The ad read:

"Walmart needs me!

Walmart employees have bad breath…

Walmart needs to carry our brush! It will sell better than anything in your store."

Within a couple of days, Jeffrey's team got an email from Walmart headquarters telling them they'd seen the ad and they could stop telling Walmart employees they have bad breath. The Orabrush team expected an invite to meet face-to-face, but the call never came. Instead, they received an email from Walmart's buyer asking if they could handle the delivery of 735,000 Orabrushes in just a few months.

Walmart had placed an order without ever talking to an Orabrush employee. And in less than two years, Orabrush had gone from zero dollars in sales and no retail distribution, to nationwide distribution and millions of dollars in sales using nothing but YouTube and a $28 Facebook ad.

Jeffrey, the MBA student who realized he could get closer to the center of his target consumer's universe, is now the CMO of Orabrush.

The Galilean Model

Jeffrey Harmon knew that trying to convince people to come to the Orabrush website to buy a product to solve a problem they didn't know they had was a losing strategy. He also understood that getting people to come to the website to realize they had an oral hygiene problem wasn't going to work, either.

Instead, he embraced the idea that creating the right kind of content on a channel close to the center of his target audience's online activities could do both: help those targets realize they had a problem *and* provide them with a solution.

Remember Ptolemy? For those of you who don't, Claudius Ptolemy was a Greek-Roman astronomer who spent decades plotting celestial constellations in the first century A.D. Ptolemy created a series of tables and charts that plotted the position of the sun, planets, and even stars as they moved across the sky. Ptolemy's model of the universe was based on a long-standing assumption that the Earth was at the center. They called this the geocentric model of the universe.

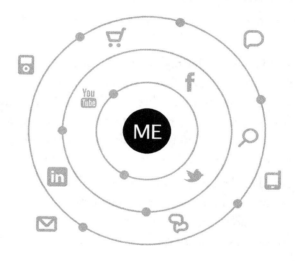

PTOLEMAIC MODEL

Figure 2: Is this how you envision your customer's online universe? With your website at the middle?

Fifteen years ago, when I got my start building websites, we all treated the web like Ptolemy viewed the astronomical universe: our website was the center of the web world. We built websites designed to include every conceivable piece of information and stored it on our domain. Customers were expected to visit our web address (our planet at the center of our web world) and find exactly what they needed. Figure 2 might still represent the prevailing world view of many of you reading this book. I know it represents the view of many of the executives I meet in my business.

Today, however, all of that has changed. Today's web world resembles the astronomical model popularized by Galileo Galilei. In 1610, Galileo began supporting a revolutionary new model of the universe—a model in which the sun sat at the center.

For more than 1,500 years, people had embraced Ptolemy's geocentric model. Galileo's heliocentric model was received with consternation and concern. The heliocentric model seemed to lessen the importance of our world by demoting the Earth to a planet like Venus or Jupiter. Galileo got a lot of flack for his model of the universe because it's hard to reset your entire worldview.

GALILEAN MODEL

Figure 3: A more accurate visualization of where you fit into your customer's online experience.

Today's web world is much more Galilean than it is Ptolemaic. You cannot continue to pour all your energy and effort into convincing consumers to come to your domain. You're no longer at the center of the universe. *Search* is at the center of today's web universe, and as you move farther and farther away from the search "sun," you travel through your consumer's most trusted, most visited websites.

Your clients travel through many different websites, news sites, blogs, Facebook friends, LinkedIn contacts, groups, Twitter, etc., before they get to your website. For the vast majority of your consumers and clients, your website is more like Pluto than the sun. There are very few brands large and powerful enough to be close to the center of the universe, and you can probably name them right off the top of your head. Think about where you and your customers spend more time— browsing your website or connecting with colleagues, leads, customers, and friends on LinkedIn and searching for information on Google?

If you live in a Galilean universe but think like Ptolemy, you end up being an isolated outlying planet where your customer rarely encounters an authentic interaction with your business. On the other hand, brands that embrace the Galilean way of thinking find themselves creating content and interacting with customers on websites much closer to the center of where those customers live. These authentic interactions, driven by the right kind of content, build new relationships and help you grow your business.

The Orabrush team was humble enough to realize they stood a greater chance to reach Walmart executives on Facebook, rather than expect those executives to visit the Orabrush website or YouTube channel. Placing extremely targeted, personalized Facebook ads made an immediate impact. This is the power of understanding the Galilean web model.

Orabrush thinks like Galileo and it's built their business. Two years after Orabrush debuted their first YouTube video, their channel had nearly 200,000 subscribers and more than 45 million video views. And they didn't stop after their initial video success. The Orabrush team has debuted a new video almost every week for two years. They've built an entertaining series with the world's largest tongue and they're committed to a focused YouTube strategy.

In a world where your website is no longer the center of the universe, Jeffery Harmon realized that to be successful "one should create a steady stream of content; it's not enough to be a one-hit wonder."[12]

You Still Need a Website

Now, at the risk of sounding like I'm contradicting myself, you still need a website. Orabrush still needs a website. Where would their customers have placed orders for the product if they didn't have a website? You just need to clearly define what role your website plays in the purchase process and have more realistic expectations for its performance.

Orabrush relied on their website to process orders instead of market the product. This was an extremely smart approach to understanding the role the website would play. The majority of consumers coming to Orabrush's website no longer needed convincing that they had a problem. Orabrush didn't need to explain the features and function of the product. Instead, they needed to convert desperate customers looking for a cure for bad breath as quickly as possible.

So, yes, you still need a website. But start thinking more like Galileo to harness the power of an ever-increasingly fragmented media landscape where your website matters less and less.

WHAT IF...

Embracing the Galilean model of the web world is a humbling experience. However, the more you insert your brand into the world of your consumers' everyday experience, the more relevant you become. This has real-world implications if you're willing to stand out in a crowd.

Penny Arcade Expo (PAX) is an amazing, intriguing, and exciting festival featuring all things gaming. From video games to board games, they have it all. Targeted at consumers, the event attracts more than 70,000 gamers.

The trade show floor is a cacophony of collaboration—people from around the world playing games with their friends. They're playing the pre-release versions of the greatest video games from the biggest manufacturers. They're playing board games and card games you've never heard of. They're staring at computer monitors and cards trying to beat their opponents.

There must be a thousand trade show booths featuring one game or another. But, at the 2011 PAX East fair, one little booth stood out from the rest. As I approached, I wondered what the 10 people standing around it looked so amused about. They weren't selling video games or joysticks. They were selling eye drops. Rohto Eyedrops to be exact. Now I'm sure Rohto goes to lots of pharmaceutical trade shows and retail events, but at those shows they're just another beauty product manufacturer. At PAX, they were an anomaly.

Sure they were giving out free samples, but they were also conducting a competition called "Stare Wars." For a bunch of gamers who stare at a computer monitor for hours without blinking this was a matter of pride. Who could stare longer? After three days, the winner was a gamer named Maxwell Morin. His stats: 54 matches, 3 hours 1 minute and 55 seconds total staring time. What did he win? A $1,500 gift card and a trip to PAX Prime in Seattle to defend his title.

Rohto isn't trying to be the eye drop for everyone. They showed up at PAX, embraced the audience and stood out from the crowd.

Why are you going to trade shows where everyone's selling the same thing to the same audience? What if you got outside your comfort zone and went to a trade show where you forced yourself to be relevant? What if you embraced the idea that you're not at the center of your customer's universe, online or off?

Ask Yourself...

Where does our audience live online?

Your audience doesn't want to constantly be dragged away from their websites of choice to visit your domain. That's a fact. I can also guarantee that no matter what industry you're in, your customers are participating somewhere you should be. (Trust me, I've found vibrant and voluminous communities of contractors and diabetics, crochet aficionados and tea drinkers—your audience is out there.)

I suggest you choose one place. Just one social media site, forum, or YouTube channel and stake a claim. Start building an audience outside your domain. But don't measure your effectiveness on that site by how many leads or click-throughs it brings to your website. Focus on building an audience of fans, followers, subscribers (or whatever they call them) on *that* channel.

(If you're already on a "bunch of social platforms," stop. Go back to the Ask Yourself section in Chapter 6 to help you identify which channel to focus on.)

It's not easy, but accepting the reality that you live in a Galilean world will change the way you interact, share, and succeed online. It all starts by asking this one simple question: Am I a Galileo or a Ptolemy?

Chapter 9
Everyone Has an Audience

We All Have a Voice

In a Galilean web world, everyone and anyone can build an audience. Those fans you have on Facebook and your followers on Twitter? That's an audience. Your competitors, partners, customers, employees, and vendors all have their own audiences, too. While you might look at this as competition, you can also look at it as an opportunity.

Let's go back a few decades to see how embracing the audiences of others can pay off big time.

Tony Bennett's Meteoric Return

In the late 1980s, Tony Bennett's career was on a downslide. Although he'd been tremendously successful in the 60s, he was now facing near financial ruin. He needed to engineer a comeback.

Tony's son Danny firmly believed that if a new generation was exposed to his dad's music they would fall in love with him, buy his albums, and return Tony to his celebrity status. But how do you convince an MTV generation to buy an album full of Frank Sinatra standards backed up by the Ralph Sharon Trio?

The traditional ad exec might have suggested Danny buy billboards in Times Square, right outside of the MTV studios, or shoot a slick commercial and buy some time on VH1. The average PR person might have called his or her contacts to offer Tony up for interviews and appearances on shows that his new target audience watched. The typical agent, brand marketer, or record executive might have suggested that Tony change his look, update his song choices, and conduct an extreme music makeover to attract a younger audience, even at the expense of his old and loyal fan base (they're dying anyway). A social media marketer (if social media had existed at the time) might have suggested that Tony join Twitter, build a Facebook fan page, start blogging, and hold a contest.

But Danny Bennett had no money. Buying advertising or posting billboards in Times Square was out of the question. Changing his father's look, music, or style wasn't an option, either. Sure, Tony could appear on talk shows and do interviews for magazines, but what was he going to talk about?

Rather than give up, Danny began to reengineer Tony's career by executing a novel marketing strategy that borrowed from advertising, branding, public relations, and even talent management. The strategy was simple: Tony would sing duets with some of the most popular artists in the world in the hopes of attracting an entirely new audience.

In 1998, I had an opportunity to see Danny Bennett's strategy in action. I had just started working with the Muppets at the Jim Henson Company in New York. One afternoon, I volunteered to be a Muppet wrangler (essentially a puppet security guard) for Elmo during an appearance on VH1. At the time, VH1 had a show called *Storytellers* on which famous musicians would chat with the audience about their lives, their inspirations, and the stories behind their songs. On this night, Elmo would be singing with none other than Tony Bennett.

Elmo and Tony sang a song off their new album, *The Playground*, and as I stood in the wings of the dimly lit studio and looked into the faces in the audience, I realized that Tony Bennett had done it. He had managed to attract an entirely new audience that crossed generations. This smiling studio audience was young and old. As an article in the *New York Times* said, "Tony Bennett has not just bridged the generation gap, he has demolished it. He has solidly connected with a younger crowd weaned on rock. And there have been no compromises."

Elmo wasn't the only guest that night on *Storytellers*. Tony also sang with The Backstreet Boys, who were wildly popular at the time.

In eight years, Tony Bennett had gone from tired Las Vegas sideshow to hip cultural icon. He had appeared on *MTV Unplugged, Late Night with Conan O'Brien, The Simpsons*, and *David Letterman* (to name a few). His unplugged album had gone platinum. He had won four more Grammy awards (to add to the two he received in 1963), an Emmy award for his performance on A&E's *Live by Request*, and had sung duets with the likes of K.D. Lang, The Dixie Chicks, James Taylor, Stevie Wonder, Paul McCartney, Christina Aguilera, and Bono. Every duet Tony recorded, exposed him to a new audience—the audience of his new singing partner.

As for Danny Bennett, he's what you'd call an expert brandscaper. Like Danny, you have to be open to new types of partnerships— partnerships with other brands whose audiences you want.

Who Owns Your Audience?

In the 1980s, and even into the 90s, Tony and Danny Bennett had no choice but to rely on traditional media to help spread the word and distribute their content. That's no longer the case. Today, anyone can implement a brandscaping strategy like Danny's. It doesn't matter if you're a local diner or a Fortune 100 company selling copiers.

We marketers no longer have to buy advertising space or time from traditional media companies in order to access our audience. We have our own audiences. They're made up of followers, fans, email newsletter subscribers, and video channel viewers. They're bloggers and photographers. They're rabid consumers and creators of content— credible, compelling, informative content that makes their jobs easier, their families happier, and their lives better.

If you don't own the audience you want, someone else does—and it's not necessarily a media company.

The Ford Fiesta Movement

We all know how it worked decades ago. Essentially, media companies created content that delivered a specific audience that companies found valuable. Businesses would find the most relevant newspaper, trade magazine, television program, or radio station, and buy advertising time or space in the hopes that the exposure would result in more sales.

Things are a lot different today for Ford Motor Company, as compared to 1964 when it announced the Ford Mustang at the New York World's Fair. That global stage kicked off a huge advertising campaign that included print ads, television and radio commercials.

For the next year, Ford built demand for the Mustang by inundating the public with teaser images of the car and intriguing ads featuring herds of horses rumbling through the West. It worked. The Mustang went on to become one of the most successful offerings in the Ford lineup.

Now compare those methods to 2010, when Ford decided to re-launch the compact Ford Fiesta after a 30-year absence in the U.S. market. Ford's approach this time around was to identify 100 online personalities (such as bloggers and YouTube content creators) to partner with. Every one of these online personalities had their own audience. They had all been delivering high-quality, relevant content on a regular basis to niche consumers who trusted their opinions and insights.

As Bud Caddell, an expert brandscaper and digital strategist with Undercurrent, the agency behind the concept, said in a 2010 interview with author Grant McCracken:

> *"The idea was: let's go find twenty-something YouTube storytellers who've learned how to earn a fan community of their own. [People] who can craft a true narrative inside video, and let's go talk to them. And let's put them inside situations that they don't get to normally experience/document. Let's add value back to their life. They're always looking, they're always hungry, they're always looking for more content to create. I think this gets things exactly right. Undercurrent grasped the underlying motive (and the real economy) at work in the digital space. People are not just telling stories for the sake of telling stories, though certainly, these stories have their own rewards. They were making narratives that would create economic value."*[13]

Ford offered each participant a 2011 Ford Fiesta to drive for six months. Each person was asked to create content that documented their experiences with the car as part of their daily life, but was also given suggestions and missions from the Ford marketing team. Ford's monthly challenges focused on unique content creation ideas, like creating a YouTube video of puppies playing soccer.

Ford worked hard to attach its brand to the constantly evolving digital landscape by understanding what kind of content would appeal to its audience. Obviously, if you're going to pick up a bunch of puppies, you'll need to fit them in your ultra-compact Ford Fiesta.

The company encouraged each participant to create content for five specific digital channels: Flickr, Twitter, Facebook, YouTube, and their own blogs. In doing so, Ford brandscaped to multiply the potential audience to more than 500 web properties (100 participants times five channels). Each of these channels is much closer to the center of their consumers' daily life than Ford's website.

Of course, Ford created a microsite, FiestaMovement.com, that compiled all the content as it was created. But they knew they'd see the effects of the content outside of the microsite. They'd see it on each individual platform created by their chosen online personalities.

In effect, Ford turned itself into an enabler of great content and invited talented participants to share it with their audiences to build brand awareness, brand equity, and drive demand for the Ford Fiesta. And drive demand it did. The Fiesta Movement was a huge success. During the first six days of the car's domestic release, Ford received 50,000 requests for the vehicle.

Leveraging Ford's Audience

Next, Ford began to share their audience with other relevant brands. This increased the reach and exposure for their content creators, and, as a result, the Ford Fiesta.

Ford meticulously broke down its talented creators' passions and created a series of niche content opportunities like travel, technology, social activism, adventure, and entertainment. Within each of these passions, they partnered with other brands to help highlight other products, services, and movements that would be relevant, exciting, and enticing to the participant's audience.

So, how do you marry a fashion-forward blogger with a Ford Fiesta and MAC makeup? You challenge your content creators to visit a MAC beauty counter and ask the beauty consultant for a Ford Fiesta-inspired makeover. The results were unusual, inspired, and eye-popping, while the marketing results were brilliant. MAC shared the videos with their fans on Facebook, Twitter, the MAC website, and through email. Ford did the same, while their content creators were exposed to an ever-growing audience.

In another challenge, Ford asked their content creators to design a Nike ID shoe like a Ford Fiesta. They partnered with Lego and challenged the geekiest content creators to build a 1/10-scale model of the Ford Fiesta. Socially conscious participants visited their local YMCAs, raised money for cancer, and even volunteered for after-school mentoring programs.

In essence, Ford's willingness to share its audience with MAC, Nike, Meals on Wheels, Lego, Hot Wheels, Habitat for Humanity, and dozens of other brands encouraged the sharing of their content on those brands' social platforms.

Sharing your audience gives you scale and reach—exactly what traditional media outlets sell. Owning an audience affords you the ability and the leverage you need to begin working with other brands that find the same audience valuable.

WHAT IF...

Duets, like the ones Tony Bennett produced, are unbelievably powerful when embraced by brands. Brandscapes don't have to just be leveraged as marketing tools; they can become product development opportunities as well. Two brands and their respective audiences can immediately generate an inherent demand for the products they create.

What if two brands got together to do exactly that? How about a car manufacturer and a watch designer?

In 1983, a new wristwatch brand hit the market. Swatch manufactured casual, fun, and relatively disposable watches in a variety of exciting colors. They were able to do this because their design team created an innovative approach to manufacturing Swatch watches. By acting on the simple idea that their watches could use fewer, interchangeable parts across all product lines, they were able to keep costs low and quality high. Swatch became an iconic 1980s brand that grew into the world's largest watch company.

By the late 1980s, the Swatch design team realized that their manufacturing innovations might be applied to other industries. So, they decided to tackle one of the most complicated manufacturing processes head-on: the automobile.

In 1994, Swatch partnered with Mercedes to concept, design, and bring to market a new kind of energy-efficient, affordable vehicle that leveraged Swatch's design and manufacturing expertise and Mercedes' automobile skill. The result became known as the Smart Car. Smart is actually an acronym for (S)watch (M)ercedes Art car.

Unfortunately, by the time the car came to market, Swatch's brand cache had waned and the Mercedes team downplayed the role the brand played in the partnership. What if Mercedes and Swatch worked together to elevate both brands? Would the Smart Car be more popular today if they'd tapped into a still rabid Swatch fan base?

What would happen if *you* leveraged brandscaping to create new product opportunities with other brands?

Ask Yourself...

Who would we want to sing a duet with?

Over the first five chapters of this book, I suggested you make a list of:

- Other brands your consumers purchase before they have a need for your product;
- Your past PR hits and the other brands or people mentioned;
- Brand advocates—people who authentically embrace your products;
- Brands that already own your audience; and
- At least a few examples of content your audience is already consuming.

Now, it's time to review and merge those lists. Find the names of the people behind those brands—the CEOs, the CMOs, the personalities who have built those brands. Find the authors of the content your audience loves and the individuals quoted in those PR hits.

This is your duet list. These are the people who you're going to brandscape with. These people, and the ones you've yet to discover, will power your success.

In the Galilean model, people power the future of your marketing efforts. Every one of the individuals on your list has an audience and it's your job to begin finding the threads that bind them. What do all of these people have in common? What do they, and their audiences, value?

Part Two
Branding in the New World

If we're going to embrace the paradigm shifts that make brandscaping possible, it's imperative that we redefine what a brand is in a new media world.

The term "brand" is a marketing relic. It's so old, in fact, that it dates back to the thirteenth century when Italians added watermarks to the paper they created to authenticate the validity of a letter's sender. To most marketers, a brand is simply the logo, name, design, or symbol that identifies one company's goods from another's.

Today, however, "brand" also refers to the *personality* of a product or a company. There are personal brands, professional brands, commodity brands, even concept brands in the marketplace today. One thing has become clear, though, in a digital world—no brand is an island.

Chapter 10
No Brand is an Island

Be Humble

Be honest. Your clients don't wake up thinking about your company, the products you sell, or the services you provide. You can try and shove your brand in front of their face using traditional advertising methods. You can invest in a PR strategy that inserts your company into today's headlines. You can churn out a bunch of content hoping to find yourself on their Facebook wall (when they check it). You can push your emails and tweet your promotional offers. But if you open your eyes to the world your consumers actually live in, you will find yourself in a more valuable position.

In the digital world, no brand is an island. Every individual builds his or her own brandscape. Your customers "like" the brands they identify with on Facebook. They "follow" the content creators they trust on Twitter. They read email newsletters from brands they've purchased from in the past. They subscribe to YouTube channels that create and distribute content they're interested in. All of this opt-in activity means you stand a better chance of finding yourself in the social stream of your potential customers if you partner with the right brands, personalities, and content creators.

Think of the digital world as an opportunity to build brand mashups.

What's a Mashup?

Mashups have proliferated in the digital world. In essence, a mashup recombines existing work to create a derivative work. There are app mashups (taking digital data from a variety of sources to create a new experience). There are video mashups (taking a variety of videos to create a new video). There are even book mashups that combine pre-existing text with a certain pop-genre (e.g., *Pride and Prejudice and Zombies*).

If you've ever listened to an album by mashup genius GirlTalk, you're already familiar with the genre. If you're not, check out this song from GirlTalk's *Feed The Animals* album (http://bit.ly/girltalkvid). The video itself lists the 15 individual songs that make up GirlTalk's mashup.

Mashups are easily accessible content. Imagine if I took 15 of your favorite songs and mashed them up to create one spectacular song. You'd probably love it. Now, imagine if I added a song you'd never heard before to the mashup. You'd probably be interested in hearing, maybe even purchasing, the original song. In fact, mashup artists will tell you that the exposure they get for the mashed-up songs actually increases sales for each individual song.

Smart brandscapers think more like mashup artists than marketers. They're always looking for brands their target audience has an existing affinity for, and they partner with those brands to get closer to their prospects. The benefits include increased relevance, exposure, and more opportunities for authentic interaction.

Gymkhana, DC Shoes, and Universal Studios

You're probably completely unaware of a subculture of auto aficionados who follow the World Rally Championship series of racing. A rally race takes place on regular roads with road-legal (albeit tricked-out) cars. Within the subculture of rally racing, there's an even more niche-focused audience of passionate people who love Gymkhana. (Take note: we're now talking about a niche within a niche.)

Gymkhana has its roots in English equestrian events. In the old days, a horse and rider would gallop around a complicated obstacle course as fast as possible to demonstrate their talents.

A few decades ago, auto testers in the U.K. decided to build obstacle courses to test the performance of their vehicles. As these courses became more and more complex, rally racers took them on to put on a show. Often, these courses include 180 and 360-degree turns. They even parallel park at breakneck speeds. Drivers must memorize the complicated course and attempt to finish faster than their counterparts. Gymkhana drivers are a special breed.

One of the most high-profile Gymkhana drivers is Ken Block. Ken drives for the Monster World Rally Team (that's Monster as in the energy drink, for which he's a brand advocate and spokesperson). He's also the co-founder and chief brand officer for a clothing manufacturer called DC Shoes (which is owned by Quicksilver).

In the rally world, Ken's a celebrity. In the fashion world, his brand's built a massive following and an $80 million business. As you can see, Ken has already built a powerful brandscape of his own. But his mashup doesn't end there. That's where it starts.

DC Shoes has always relied on a heavy dose of video content to embrace the lifestyle of its skateboarding, snowboarding, rally fans. With almost 400 videos and 200,000 subscribers, its YouTube channel is a pop-culture force.

In August 2011, Ken released a new YouTube video that demonstrated his brandscaping chops. It wasn't Ken's first Gymkhana video. It was actually his fourth in a series of mega-productions that feel more like mini feature films rather than demonstrations of his driving talent. The fourth video is aptly titled *Gymkhana Four: The Hollywood Megamercial.*

During the nine-minute masterpiece, shot on the Universal Studios backlot, Ken Block, wearing DC Shoes, drives his tricked-out 2011 Ford Fiesta—emblazoned with the Monster Energy and Mobil logos—past robotic sharks, deranged zombies, through soundstages, and runs circles around a stoic gorilla on a jet-powered Segway. The film is directed by Ben Conrad, a Hollywood insider, and even features a cameo by YouTube sensation Epic Meal Time. (Go ahead, watch the video, you won't be disappointed – http://bit.ly/Gymkhana4Video.)

Now before you read any further, re-read that last paragraph and count the brands that appear in this one video. I count nine. *Nine* other brands. (Remember to include personal brands because in a digital world everyone has an audience.)

Essentially, every single one of these brands is mashed up as part of the content. Presented in this context, every brand takes on a new meaning to the audience that's consuming it, and as the video is distributed, every brand is exposed to each other's audience. Let me tell you, the Ford Fiesta never looked so powerful, so fun, so agile, and so cool.

Gymkhana Four was viewed more than 18 million times in 11 months. It's been written about on more than 1 million websites around the world. A quick look at the list of media coverage reveals that everyone from *AutoWeek, ESPN,* and *GamersHell* to *USA Today* and *Adweek* picked up the content and made it relevant to their respective audiences. As a whole, Ken Block's first three Gymkhana videos garnered 110 million video views. That's a brandscape I'd want to be part of.[14]

While you've probably heard of Monster Energy, Ford, Universal Studios, and Mobil, you've probably never heard of Epic Meal Time. But the fact is, Epic Meal Time did more than Ford, Universal Studios, and Mobil combined to bring a new audience to the Gymkhana world.

Everything's Better with Bacon

Epic Meal Time is a YouTube cooking show known for creating an extremely gross meal online every Tuesday. It's disgusting and definitely not for the faint of heart (or anyone who's even mildly health-conscious). Their meal creations include a Fast Food Pizza, the Massive Meat Log, and the Meatball Deathstar. Each recipe integrates pounds of bacon and shots of Jack Daniels. The show's host, Harley Morenstein, uses foul language (bleeped out by screeching crow calls) and hip hop slang.

Just to give you a flavor of their creations, let me run down the ingredients for the Fast Food Pizza: KFC Popcorn Chicken, a Taco Bell Crunchwrap Supreme (taco), a McDonald's Big Mac and Chicken McNuggets, a Wendy's Baconator and french fries, an A&W Teen Burger (bacon cheeseburger) and onion rings, on top of a cheese pizza. It's enough to make you gag. Every episode ends with Harley and his team of misfits chowing down their monstrous creation. (http://bit.ly/EpicMealtime)

It doesn't matter what you (or I) think of the content, the Epic Meal Time crew has built an audience of more than 2.3 million subscribers and has generated nearly 400 million video views from males between the ages of 13 and 34. This is the audience Ken Block and Ford want to reach. It's exactly the audience that would embrace Gymkhana, buy a Ford Fiesta, and wear DC Shoes. That's exactly why Ken invited them to build a set in the middle of the Universal Studios lot and appear as a cameo in *Gymkhana Four.*

Four minutes and 15 seconds into *Gymkhana Four,* Ken drives his Ford Fiesta around Harley and the Epic Meal Time crew while they appear to be shooting an episode of their show. Ten seconds later, they're gone. In a 10-minute video, we see the Epic Meal Time crew for exactly 10 seconds.

However, four days before Ken Block released *Gymkhana Four* on YouTube, the Epic Meal Time gang released a video for their audience hyping up their cameo in Ken Block's DC Shoes Film. They tweeted about it (to their few hundred thousand followers) and they wrote about it on their website. During those four days leading up to the Gymkhana video release, the Epic Meal Time crew garnered more than 100,000 views for their teaser video. They created a hype storm that generated 1,000 online articles on websites like Edmunds.com and Facebook.

Harley's Epic Meal Time crew had successfully married their audience with Ken Block's audience to build momentum and anticipation for the release of *Gymkhana Four.*

Now why would Epic Meal Time agree (I imagine for free) to be part of Ken Block's video? For the exact same reason Ken wanted them to be part of his video: they saw the opportunity to reach an entirely untapped audience of like-minded consumers already attached to the DC Shoes brand. This is a social media symbiotic relationship in action—this is the power of thinking like a brandscaper.

Mutually Beneficial Relationships

Because Ford partnered with Ken Block and Ken Block partnered with Epic Meal Time, Ford found itself relevant to an audience that has an affinity for over-the-top fast-food meals, bacon, and Jack Daniels. That's smart brandscaping.

You don't have to be a Ford, a DC Shoes, or even a Universal Studios to be a good brandscaper. All you have to do is open your mind to the opportunities that exist with powerful content creators who already reach your audience.

Webinars, Authors, and Software

Consider the content creation and partnership efforts of Awareness, Inc., which sells B2B social media software solutions.

Every other week, Mike Lewis, vice president of marketing and sales for Awareness, hosts an educational webinar. The webinar has nothing to do with software. Instead, they invite well-respected marketers and authors to speak on a topic relevant to the Awareness audience of social media marketers.

Each guest promotes that they're going to appear on an Awareness webinar. They include it in their email newsletter. They tweet their followers. They post the appearance on their Facebook page. They invite their publishers, friends, and family members. They even invite members from the LinkedIn groups in which they participate.

It's a mutually beneficial relationship. The author gets exposure for his or her book, and Awareness gets access to the author's audience to help sell its services. Meanwhile, the audience gets access to great content and insight from some of the most well-respected thought leaders in the business.

As Mike Lewis points out, "It's not just about acquiring new customers; it's actually great for nurturing new customers and leads through the buying process. The webinars have touched every aspect of our sales cycle."

The webinars have been so successful in generating book sales for the authors, that publishers such as Wiley and McGraw-Hill now have relationships with Awareness, too.

It doesn't matter if you're a software provider, an automaker, an entertainment act, or a shoemaker—you can develop two-way, symbiotic, content-based relationships that can open up all kinds of new doors for your business. And you don't have to spend a dime on traditional advertising or public relations to do it.

WHAT IF...

Starbucks recently unveiled a new line of blended frozen beverages called Frappuccinos. The accompanying advertising campaign touts the "anyway-you-want-it" virtues of ordering your own version of the drink using all sorts of flavors, coffee, toppings, and syrups. Essentially, Starbucks is selling frozen-drink mashups.

What if Starbucks created music mashups to promote their new drinks?

As an *Adweek* article revealed, Starbucks is targeting consumers between the ages of 18 to 25 with their new coffee concoction campaign.[15]

The A.V. Club (AVClub.com) reaches tons of 18 to 25-year-olds every month (about 2.5 million of them) by producing high-quality, entertaining, pop-culture content. They even have a whole section dedicated to music.

So what does the A.V. Club and Starbucks have in common? The desire to reach the same audience. Sure, they could have just bought a bunch of display ads, but instead Starbucks decided to fund the creation of 25 cover songs and music videos.

Every week, a famous band (like Ben Folds or They Might Be Giants) is invited into the A.V. Club's "round room," to sing their take on a famous tune (like something from the Beach Boys or Bruce Springsteen). They're familiar songs, sung in new ways—just like the Frappuccino's familiar flavors blended into new combinations. They called the show *AV Undercover: brought to you by Starbucks' Frappuccino*.

By 2012, *AV Undercover* started its third season sponsored by Starbucks, which has reached 1.2 million viewers through the show. It's a perfect blend of musical talent, familiar songs, and wonderful fun, all brought to the viewer by a logical sponsor.

What's even more interesting is that each and every one of the cover bands has also promoted the release of each video in an authentic way to their extremely large audiences, which helps *AV Undercover* and Starbucks extend their reach and their relationship with their target audience even farther.

Starbucks, A.V. Club, and the participating bands have all benefitted by embracing their respective audiences. What if you created your own industry mashup? What if you welcomed the audiences of other brands? What kind of content would you create?

Ask Yourself...

What can we do to demonstrate the power of our audience?

Your audience is powerful. They've got cash to spend on other products and services you believe in, support, and recommend. In the eyes of your customers, you're a trusted source. They've made a commitment to buy your products because you've earned it.

Look down your list of potential brandscape partners and pick three or four brands you believe in the most. As you consume their content, keep your eye out for the stuff your audience would appreciate, understand, and embrace.

When (or if) you find some great content, reach out to the brand and ask them if you can distribute it to your audience. Who's gonna say no to an invitation like that? Don't copy the content onto your website (that's Ptolemaic thinking)—endorse and contextualize it for your audience and invite them to consume what your brandscape partner has created, where they created it.

If your audience is motivated to take action, your newfound partner will know it. Ask them if they saw any demonstrable impact in their business. Did they sell more products that day (or the days following)? Did they generate any valuable leads? Did your audience make any other impact on their business? If the answer's yes, it's time to sit down and start talking about a deeper, longer-term brandscaping relationship.

No brand is an island and everyone has an audience. Ask yourself how powerful your audience is.

Note: If your audience doesn't make a discernable impact, that's okay. It just means you have some work to do. Go back to setting an expectation for your audience and building a trusted relationship with them through valuable content.

Chapter 11
Social Branding is Personal

Show Your Face

When *TIME* magazine named "You—Yes, You" as its prestigious person of the year, more marketers should have stood up and taken notice.

While the American Marketing Association still defines a brand as a "name, term, design, symbol, or any other feature that identifies one seller's goods or service as distinct from those of other sellers," any social media-savvy marketer knows that the brands of the future are people-powered.

Social media is driven by social interaction. The actual definition of social interaction is "an interpersonal relationship between two or more people that may range from fleeting to enduring..."

It's not possible to have a social interaction with a brand. It's incredibly inauthentic. No matter how much I love a brand, the notion that I can have a meaningful "interpersonal relationship" with a brand is idiotic.

But I *can* have a relationship—a deep, meaningful relationship— leveraging today's social media, with a person *from* a brand. This leads me to believe that even the largest brands in the future will be people-powered.

People are the Brand

Imagine if you attended a corporate networking event, a cocktail hour at a convention, or even a job fair, and you had the option of talking to two people: one person identifies himself as "Joe Tripodi, CMO, Coca-Cola." The other person simply wears a name tag that says "Coca-Cola." Which person do you want to connect with? Share a beer with? Learn from? I'm sure it's Joe—not the giant brand Coca-Cola.

Too many brands treat their social media platforms like traditional advertising and promotion distribution opportunities. Coca-Cola's "official" tweet stream is an unending list of attempts to feign a personality for the brand. "Good luck with your report, Julie," was a tweet delivered to a Florida State University (FSU) student who tweeted, "Writing a report on @CocaCola while drinking #CocaCola..."

Wouldn't it have been much more meaningful if Joe himself had tweeted the exact same thing?

How psyched would a young sports management student ("considering a double major in advertising or marketing") have been if the CMO of a legendary brand had reached out to help her finish her paper on "gendered messages in advertising"? How many people at FSU would have heard about her "personal" encounter with a Fortune 500 CMO? I doubt anyone cared that a nameless, faceless, logo tweeted back a few words of encouragement. As far as I can tell, Joe Tripodi doesn't even have a Twitter account.

If Coca-Cola really believes it can "refresh the world" and "inspire moments of optimism and happiness..." as its mission statement says, don't you think an authentic, refreshing, inspirational, and personal moment could have been created with a tweet?

Meanwhile, brands like Zappos, Dell, and even GE have completely embraced the notion of the individual as an extension of the brand. Their CMOs are accessible on Twitter, answering even mundane questions that give life and personality to their brands. Those are brands I connect with, literally. I connect with them through the people behind the brand. Go ahead, tweet @BethComstock, GE's CMO. She'll respond, as long as the tweet is relevant.

In a world where we can connect with the people behind a brand, who wants to have a relationship with a nameless, faceless brand?

This is how social media works. It's no different than a cocktail party or a networking event, with one notable exception: Social media has given your individual brand scale. One social interaction with a student becomes an opportunity to showcase your brand's commitment to "inspire moments of optimism and happiness."

Welcome to the new age of corporate branding where the sum of the people that make up your brand is more powerful than a logo. Welcome to the power of the individual brandscaper.

Talent Fuels Your Success

If all brands are intrinsically people-powered, no brand is an island, and everyone has an audience, it's time to consider how you can leverage any individual's brand to add personality, scale, and reach to your company's marketing efforts.

Lauren Luke is the personality that powers her brand. Tom Dickson is the authentic persona that drives Blendtec's blender sales. Ken Block propels DC Shoes' brand. Every content creator for the Ford Fiesta Movement adds life and builds content that drives social interactions around a myriad of brands.

Choosing the right personality to attach to your brand for the long term is no easy task. In the television business, the personalities that represent a show are called the "talent." For example, Alex Trebek is the talent for *Jeopardy*. The talent you attach to your brand is just as important as the brand itself. Blendtec intrinsically understood this.

The team at Blendtec could have hired some young, hip guy to host its video show. Choosing someone representative of the target market might have been the logical choice for attracting an audience. Or they could've hired some comely spokesmodel designed to attract the attention of the demographic they knew held the purchase power in the marketplace. Instead, they turned to their middle-aged CEO and founder Tom Dickson.

Tom Dickson isn't the most attractive, dynamic, or exciting choice of hosts (no offense, Tom), but he is the most authentic. After all, Tom invented the Blendtec blender. He's the one who started testing his invention with bizarre blends to prove its power and durability. I don't see the CEOs of Cuisinart and KitchenAid putting on lab coats and safety goggles and stepping into a test kitchen to prove that they stand behind *their* products. The *Will it Blend?* series works because people can relate to Tom.

Scaling Internal Talent

The first place to look for talent to power your brand is inside your own company. Everyone in your company has talent. Your employees are experts in your business. They're knowledgeable, insightful, and are some of the few people in the world who think about your business each and every day. They're on the front lines. They know what the customer is thinking—what their problems and challenges are. They know the competition and they see the trends.

So many companies have told me over the years that their most valuable asset is the people they've hired. If that's the case, digital media has given you the ability to put your most valuable asset to work. The world wide web and social media have handed you the ability to scale and share that insight in order to dramatically grow your business.

When people come to work for your company, they're bringing their talent to your brand. It's a partnership—a brandscape. What are you doing to encourage the evolution and growth of their individual brand? Obviously, they're also getting access to your brand's audience. They get the credibility, the heritage, and the history of your organization's success added to their brandscape as well. (They're going to put your brand name on their resume, aren't they?) It's a symbiotic relationship where both brands benefit.

Consider Indium, a company that sells soldering supplies to global electronics manufacturers. Indium's marketing team has had tremendous success by asking internal talent to share their knowledge, experience, and expertise with the engineers who buy their products. The Indium blog is a deep resource designed to help solve the challenges engineers face in the electronics business.

Indium doesn't have one or two blogs, they have 73. Each blog is powered by a person (the "talent") who's focused on a specific area of engineering. If every Indium blogger attracted an audience of 50 people per post, that would be 3,700 readers total. It adds up fast.

One of Indium's bloggers is Andy C. Mackie, a guy with a Ph.D. in physical chemistry, who shares his expertise on semiconductor assembly. His content is authentic and never self-serving. Every post he writes includes his bio, his picture, and his contact information. He's accessible. He's someone I can identify with, build a relationship with. He's someone I can subscribe to (via an RSS feed or email). And Andy's built himself an audience for his content.

Indium's been so successful building business this way that it's registered the trademark "From One Engineer to Another." Indium employees are now "celebrities" in their space.

Indium isn't a nameless, faceless, technology company. It's a company made up of real people, sharing their advice, insight, and expertise with people who need it. Indium is a social brand, powered by people.

If the future of all branding is personal, the success or failure of brandscapers' marketing efforts will rely on their ability to extend the reach of their internal talent, thought leadership, and the people who buy and sell their products or services. We must spend more time, energy, and effort helping to cultivate the personal brands of those who've already made us a success. Social success isn't manufactured—it's earned by building trust between people, not brands.

What are you doing to elevate the people who make your brand inherently social?

WHAT IF...

A few years ago, a Floridian named Jason Sadler took his personal brand and the social media audience he'd garnered and turned it into a marketing services business. Unlike most agencies in the social space, Jason didn't offer consulting services or campaign design. All he did was sell access to his personal brand and the army of individuals his videos, photos, tweets, and status updates had garnered. He sold access to his audience. (Sounds more like a media company than an agency to me.) If the future of all branding is personal, then Jason Sadler is the poster boy.

It all started when Jason woke up one morning, put on a logo-laden t-shirt, and said to himself, "If I'm going to have to put a shirt on every morning, I may as well try to get paid for it, right?"[16] And so it began.

Jason launched a website called IWearYourShirt.com. For a fee, companies purchased the opportunity for Jason to wear their t-shirt for one day. With your shirt on, Jason would post images on Flickr, videos on YouTube, host his live show on Ustream, and update his daily adventures on Twitter and Facebook. Basically, Jason turned into a walking virtual billboard.

Jason didn't just wear a shirt, though. He did his homework on each company and would walk around discussing its virtues. It worked for all kinds of brands—everything ranging from Arizona Iced Tea to Mitsubishi Electric.

Jason sold out his first year of "chest-space." His human-billboard turned social-media advertising agency had been a success. But how do you scale a business that relies on a personal brand as the advertising platform? You find more personal brands worth selling.

That's exactly what Jason did. By 2011, Jason had five t-shirt wearing, social-media personalities all willing to "wear *your* shirt."

By 2012, Jason's business had boomed and in an effort to respond to his sponsors' desire for more, longer-term social-media interactions and deeper content creation, he stopped selling day-long opportunities and started selling week-long engagements only.

Jason Sadler turned his personal brand into a media company creating valuable, sharable content for the companies he serviced. Jason Sadler represents a dramatic shift in the media landscape, one that each and every corporation can leverage for itself.

In 2009, the first full year of his grand experiment, Jason brandscaped with 365 brands willing to buy access to his audience and content to support their digital efforts. Jason is a talented, smart, and innovative brandscaper.

What if you built a business around the audience of your employees? What would it look like? What would the impact be on your business? What if you leveraged the audiences behind the personal brands that have built *your* business?

Ask Yourself

What are we doing to scale the reach of the people who power our brand?

Defiance, a powdered milk company, was having a really hard time penetrating a crowded market against 300 other brands. They'd tried advertising, but it didn't seem to sell more dried milk.

The advertisements *did* spark thousands of consumer inquiries on how to take care of a newborn baby. Instead of ignoring those inquiries, the CEO Joe Nathan hired Nurse Kennedy to answer every consumer inquiry on behalf of the company.

Word got out that Defiance would answer any infant health-related question, and before they knew it, Nurse Kennedy's staff of 11 nurses answered hundreds of questions a day. They also started selling more and more powdered milk.

That's when Defiance got smart. They published a book for new mothers that answered every single question they'd been asked. (Only one question was related to powdered milk, by the way.) They scaled their internal knowledge and the people who powered their brand by turning it into a book. Powdered milk sales skyrocketed and they distributed millions of copies of their baby book.

That company went on to become Glaxo and that book was first published in 1908. That's right, Glaxo Smith Kline, the third largest pharmaceutical company in the world (worth more than $73 billion today), owes its century-long success to Nurse Kennedy and the *Glaxo Baby Book*.

What are *you* doing to scale your salespeople's insight and understanding of their customers' needs? What are you doing to showcase the people who power your brand? Who's your Nurse Kennedy?

Chapter 12
Become a Talent Scout

The Digital Scout

By now, we should all be thinking past the one-hit-wonder mentality propagated by the public relations and advertising industry. Good brandscapers question the value of a single mention in a magazine or on a mommy blog. Instead, we should be looking for talent. We should be scouring blogs, reading news sources, listening to podcasts, and watching YouTube videos, all with one thing in mind: Who can we partner with to drive demand for our products and services? And who could *we* help scale their reach for the content they create?

In today's world, you need to become a digital talent scout. You need to identify people who are creating unique content, have an interesting angle or perspective, and have a real talent for communicating to (and with) an audience. Your goal should be to find "the next big thing"— an up-and-coming content creator who has hopes and ambitions—and explore ways you can help this person cultivate his or her talent. If you do this right, you'll reap the rewards of being intimately attached to the talent's success.

Shoes, Music, and a Struggling Industry

It's no secret that musicians create fashion trends. If you can get musicians to authentically embrace your shoes, hats, jewelry, makeup, or jeans, you can sell more. Converse knows this. Lots of famous musicians have worn (or still wear) Converse shoes: Nirvana's front man Kurt Cobain, teen pop sensation Justin Bieber, Guns & Roses guitarist Slash, and rap star Lil' Wayne, just to name a few.

A few years back, Converse got the idea to become a talent scout and brandscape with musicians *before* they hit the big time. In July 2011, Geoff Cottrill, Converse's CMO, opened a state-of-the-art recording studio in an old dry cleaning facility in Brooklyn, New York. The studio, which Converse branded Rubber Tracks, is billed as a "community-based" recording studio. It's a place where emerging bands can record their songs at no cost. What's the catch? There is none.

All artists who record at Rubber Tracks have the option to have their music promoted on Converse's website and social media channels. For a struggling band, exposing your music to Converse's 24 million Facebook fans, 50,000 Twitter followers, or 500,000 monthly website visitors is an appealing offer. In fact, Geoff describes the size of Converse's digital audience as a "decent-sized country."

Bands apply online for the opportunity to record at Rubber Tracks. Five or six acts a week are chosen to secure recording time. "The acts are selected less for their talent than for their viral energies—their presence on MySpace or Facebook, their hustle pursuing their careers..." wrote *New York Times* journalist John Leland, who covered the studio launch.[17]

Each artist is given a day or two of studio time to record up to five songs. Rubber Tracks provides the band with everything it needs, including a staff of talented engineers, instruments, and as much free Converse gear as they want.

What do the artists think of the studio? Ra Ra Riot's Rebecca Zeller says, "Knowing how hard it is to make a living as a musician and the amount of money it takes to get into a studio of that caliber, it's unbelievably generous for Converse to provide it for free...Coupled with the fact that artists retain all rights to their music is a testament to Converse."[18]

But Converse isn't just recording the music. It also creates videos about the bands and gives them exposure to Converse fans, friends, followers, and customers. According to Cottrill, Rubber Tracks gives bands "the means to expose their music to a much larger audience through compelling content captured at the studio, including exclusive in-studio video testimonials, track-of-the-week features, behind-the-scenes footage, and unique rehearsal session clips... [It's] a catalyst for creativity and provides a window to see into an artist's experience."[19]

Graffiti and Guitars

Before Converse started drawing musicians into the Rubber Tracks studio, they put a lot of effort into getting the space ready for prime time. During that time, they partnered with other brands to extend the brandscape even further.

Instead of just hanging a sign on the building, the Converse team collaborated with two of the most well-respected graffiti artists in the world. Mr. EwokOne created a massive mural on the studio's exterior. Shepard Fairey, who created the famous Barack Obama "Hope" poster, designed an original piece of art for the interior. By working with these two artists, Converse found itself part of the online community of graffiti fans.

Rather than going out and buying all the necessary gear to outfit the studio, Geoff Cottrill decided to partner with a brand that would also love to build deeper relationships with up-and-coming musicians, Guitar Center. Everything in the studio that you can strum, tap, or tune came from Guitar Center, the largest retail chain of musical instruments in the world.

Is Geoff looking for the next breakout artist? I'm sure he is. But to him it doesn't seem to matter if they find it.

"Let's say over the next five years we put 1,000 artists through here, and one becomes the next Radiohead," he said in a *New York Times* interview. "They're going to have all the big brands chasing them to sponsor their tour. But the 999 artists who don't make it, the ones who tend to get forgotten about, they'll never forget us."[20]

And for the one band that *does* "make it," Converse was there first.

Converse has become a champion of the arts in a way that feels more like the art patrons of old. During the Renaissance, it was impossible to make a living as an artist. Wealthy and powerful patrons would hire an artist or commission a specific piece ranging from portraits to landscapes and everything in between. That's how artists survived and thrived.

Brands like Converse are today's patrons. Converse understands that its support of the arts—whether it be through music or the paintings on the walls—makes its brand successful.

No Studio? No Problem

You don't have to build a studio to become a digital talent scout. With the proliferation of individual content creators in the online world, you just need to *think* like Converse to succeed like Converse. You need to forge relationships with those who are already creating content by understanding their dreams and ambitions.

Start mining YouTube and Twitter. Start looking for bloggers, podcasters, and even photographers who are creating great content. Check Vimeo (an artsy YouTube) for video content creators who might have a talent for telling a story—maybe even stories relevant to your audience. At every conference, trade show, and event you attend, look for the personalities in your industry. Find out what kind of content they're already creating—or better yet, what kind of content they'd love to create. Show them how you can help. Surely you must have corporate resources—advice, insight, or data—that can contribute to their success.

There's no magic formula for finding new talent. It's like dating—you'll know it when you see it. But you have to start looking. Leave no digital stone unturned. The talent's out there.

WHAT IF...

Guitar Center is an interesting brand—one with deep content partnerships that all revolve around showcasing the music they know their audience adores. If there's one thing you might notice about Guitar Center's brandscape with Converse, it's that Guitar Center never shares any of the Converse Rubber Track content. Why not? What if Guitar Center shared Rubber Track's weekly videos with their 400,000 Facebook fans? Wouldn't both brands benefit? Wouldn't the artists be exposed to even more people? Couldn't Guitar Center even point out what instruments the band is playing?

Let's take it a step further. Guitar Center has a partnership with DirecTV, which has nearly 20 million subscribers. DirecTV has a channel called the *Audience Network*. The channel is dedicated to showcasing original programming you won't find anywhere else, including a show sponsored (and shot) by Guitar Center. The show is called *Sessions*.

Sessions features popular bands like Plain White T's, New Found Glory, Carolina Liar, and Seether—not necessarily household names, but certainly bands bigger than the ones recording at Converse's Rubber Tracks. What if Guitar Center paired up bands that have recorded at Rubber Tracks with similar sounding, more popular bands, and invited them to perform together on *Sessions*? *Sessions* would get a new audience (Converse's) and Converse would benefit from increased exposure for the bands that wear their stuff. Maybe Converse and Guitar Center should split the bill. Each brand would get greater reach at half the cost. That's brandscaping math at work.

Ask Yourself...

What kind of talent can we work with to make our brand more relevant, more often?

You're probably not looking for the next big pop star. (Although, my firm has actually helped an appliance manufacturer leverage the power of music brandscapes to increase their reach.) So, what kind of talent should you look for? And where do you start?

A good place to begin is with your list of authentic brand advocates—people who are already out there creating content about your brand. Do they share the same values as your company? Do they speak to your audience frequently enough to drive long-term success? Do they have a knack for creating compelling content, whether it's about your brand or not?

Start consuming their content and sharing it with your audience on a regular basis. If your audience begins to embrace the content, you've discovered someone worth brandscaping with. Reach out. Ask these potential partners what you can do to help them expand or improve their content and the audience they reach. Ask them how you can help them grow their business.

Becoming a digital talent scout doesn't take a lot of time and effort. It takes a long-term commitment to finding authentic brand advocates that reach a valuable audience.

Ask yourself, who can I help expand their reach? Remember, a rising tide lifts all ships.

Chapter 13
Explore Your Customer's Brandscape

All Natural Brand Partnerships

If you've ever shopped at Amazon or rented a movie from Netflix, you know the power of the "you might also like" phenomenon. Essentially, Amazon and Netflix use your browsing, renting, and purchasing history to suggest products or movies you might also enjoy. It's amazing how accurate the algorithms that generate these suggestions are. Amazon and Netflix have come to understand your preferences and habits—they're experts at driving revenue by building brandscapes.

Think about how Converse has built a powerful brandscape. They've identified an audience that drives demand for their shoes: ambitious musicians. They dove into the musician's world to understand their Galilean universe (these musicians spend time at sites such as MySpace, Facebook, and Bandcamp). They identified where the musicians purchased their gear (Guitar Center) and noticed an appreciation for graffiti.

This is the power of understanding the audience-first approach to building deeper relationships with your consumers. Embracing, partnering, and sharing content created by your brandscaping partners can deliver big results. However, don't confuse brandscaping with co-branding. Co-branding is when two companies form an alliance to exploit a marketing synergy. Brandscaping is also not the same as co-sponsoring. Co-branding and co-sponsorships tend to be superficial marketing relationships created and dissolved as it suits the brands involved.

Brandscaping is deeper than that. Brandscapes are audience-driven. They result from the realization of the natural brand partnerships that exist in the marketplace.

When brandscapes work together to create content that's relevant to the entire audience, everyone wins. A smart brandscape actually allows you to create content with companies you might initially consider competitors for your audience's attention. Why not make that battle for attention work for you both?

You don't have to sell consumer products, trendy shoes, or slick guitars to leverage the power of brandscaping—it works for B2B audiences, too. Read on.

Move it!

If you manufacture a product in a factory, you have to get that product to your customers and retailers. If you sell products directly to consumers from your website, you have to pick, pack, and ship every order. You want to make sure your shipments aren't delayed and that everything is moving as efficiently and as cost-effectively as possible. This is the primary job of a logistics or operations person—and it's a tough job.

If you're an executive-level logistics or operations manager, you probably read the industry's premier magazine, *DC Velocity*. Browse through an issue and you'll see companies pitching pallets, forklifts, conveyors, consulting services, software, and all kinds of related products. But what logistics managers really want to know about are the *systems* their peers use to move product.

What if a bunch of these brands, competing for audience attention, joined forces to show customers how other logistics managers build efficient shipping solutions? What if they partnered to build content based on a brandscape? Well, they did.

DC Velocity brought together seven seemingly competitive brands (ranging from conveyor manufacturers to trucking companies to consultants) to create a monthly, 30-minute video show called *Move it!* The show is modeled after programs like *Extreme Engineering* and *MegaStructures* and features Steve Thomas, former host of PBS's *This Old House*, as the "talent." *DC Velocity* is the producer and serves as the brand intermediary and primary distributor—its editorial team ensures that the content is compelling and brings its audience of monthly readers to watch the show at a dedicated, neutral website (http://www.moveitshow.com).

"Have you ever wondered how all the stuff you use everyday gets to you?" asks the narrator in the pilot episode of *Move it!* "We'll find out how Amway processes half a billion dollars worth of products each year!"

Move it! is wonderfully produced. It's not for everyone, but then again, it's not supposed to be. The show is entertaining enough to capture almost anyone's attention, but detailed enough to help any logistics executive understand how some of the biggest, best, and most innovative companies make their warehouses work.

To be clear, the show is *not* a case study for any single company that contributed to make the content possible. It's a good show that tells interesting stories, with the audience's content needs as its first priority.

It's too early to know if *Move it!* is driving business for its brandscape partners, but early reactions were so good that all the brands involved wanted to do more episodes.

Every brand that took part in *Move it!* could have hired its own production company to create boring case studies about how its product makes a logistics manager's job easier. Instead, they pooled their resources to create informative and entertaining content that their audience really wants and needs.

Finding Neutral Ground

Get over yourself and your brand. Your customers don't live in a singularly branded world. They build their own brandscapes. They work with their favorite consultants. They eat their favorite cereal. They use their favorite hair care products and they go to their favorite restaurants. They're not thinking about you all the time. They're thinking about and encountering hundreds of brands every day.

Think about your typical customer for a minute. Are they Mac people or Windows people? Do they listen to country music or heavy metal? Do they wear Converse, Adidas, or Cole Haan?

Think about the businesses you visit on your sales calls. What software do they use? What kind of coffee machine is in their corporate kitchen? What brand of printers do they own? How is their office furnished?

Start tracking the trends across your customers and begin looking for brandscaping opportunities. Just because one of your customers drinks tea every day and collects bobbleheads doesn't mean it's an opportunity. But if 100 customers collect bobbleheads, start looking for ways to get in front of the rest of the bobblehead community. The best route to those customers is through a brand they already trust.

Whenever you start working with other brands to create content that benefits everyone, you need to consider where the content will live. Will it be on your website or theirs? What about both? Finding a neutral ground in the digital world has never been easier. If you're creating video, start a neutral YouTube channel. Both of you can embed video and measure your impact on viewership. If you're creating text, consider a neutral Tumblog (on Tumblr). You don't have to build a microsite. You don't have to put it on your server. Remember, you live in a Galilean universe. Content can live anywhere. The brands involved in *Move it!* leveraged the *DC Velocity* brand and their ability to host the content on a neutral channel. Get creative.

In today's marketplace, almost all publishers (traditional magazines or digital content hubs) provide brandscapers with neutral territory to launch and extend content designed to attract a shared audience. But you don't have to work with a publisher like *DC Velocity*. (Remember, don't get roped into a straight-up advertising buy either.)

A great brandscaper knows that any social media channel can become neutral territory for your content. Explore your customers' existing brandscapes to uncover the best places to distribute your content and which brand partners will add the most value.

WHAT IF...

Amazon is really good at cross-selling and merchandising on their ecommerce platform. Their algorithms analyze millions of purchases to find trends and make new recommendations based on their volume of historic purchase data. What if you leveraged Amazon's algorithms to start building your own brandscape? What if Amazon helped you explore your customer's brandscape?

Intuit sells accounting and tax software to small businesses and accountants. An Amazon search for QuickBooks, one of their marquee products, provides us with a long list of potential brandscape partners. Under the heading, "Customers who bought this item also bought," we see recommendations for NeatDesk (a desktop scanner often used for receipts); a variety of fax machines and printers from brands including Brother and Epson; Norton Antivirus software; and even printable label sheets (also from Epson).

Looking at this list, we can put ourselves in the shoes of the typical QuickBooks customer. Those customers might be setting up their new office. They need accounting software, a receipt scanner, labels for their files, an antivirus program, and even books like *Bookkeepers' Boot Camp: Get a Grip on Accounting Basics* by Angie Mohr.

So, whether you're Intuit, NeatDesk, Norton, or author Angie Mohr, you're ready to begin leveraging the audiences of the brands you've discovered using a tool available to all of us: Amazon's intelligent algorithms.

Ask Yourself...

What advertisers spend money in the trade magazines our audience reads?

One of the easiest ways to begin building your target list of brandscape partners is to explore the wide-array of advertisers in the publications your audience reads. They don't even have to be the trade magazines you advertise in.

For example, if you advertise in *Modern Manufacturing* because you sell conveyor belts, your audience probably also reads *Packaging Magazine*. Subscribe and start paying attention to the other brands targeting the manufacturing executive. You're all fighting for his or her attention; start looking for opportunities to work together. Will partnering with a few of these brands to create relevant content improve the quality of your leads?

Chapter 14
Brand Your Content

Building a Content Brand

You, your talent, and your brandscape partners need to spend considerable time and effort branding the content you create in a way that works for everyone.

When you buy advertising, whether you're buying a magazine ad or a television spot, you're buying into a content brand. If you're buying a spot on a television show, like Rachel Ray's *30 Minute Meals*, you're buying into the audience Rachel has built as the *30 Minute Meals* guru. In the digital world, you have an opportunity to build and brand your own content.

Content that's designed to be a brand on its own is far more successful and sustainable than branded content. That sounds like a subtle distinction, but blatantly branded content, emblazoned with your product, isn't as sharable, consumable, or interesting as content that happens to be brought to the audience by your brand.

It's the difference between NOVA, brought to you by Exxon Mobil, and an infomercial for the Snuggie. Sure, the Snuggie made a big splash as a gimmick gift (and I'm sure they made a lot of money), but no one watches the Snuggie infomercial anymore. Millions of people are still watching NOVA.

Most brands treat their content like a Snuggie instead of a NOVA.

You watch television shows because the content is designed for you—not because the show was designed for the advertiser. Successful brandscapers create and brand content for the audience they're trying to attract.

Blendtec doesn't call its show *Blendtec's Amazing Blender Show*. No, it's called *Will It Blend?* The Advertising Specialty Institute (ASI) doesn't call its show *The ASI Show*. They've branded it *The Joe Show*. Lauren Luke's books are called *Lauren Luke Looks*, not *Sephora's*

Makeup Tutorials. Creatively branded content helps build a relationship with the audience.

Before the digital distribution revolution, companies didn't have to think about how they branded their content. Media companies did that for you. Today, that's all changed. You need to build a content brand.

A Gem of an Idea

Project Runway is a reality television show that features aspiring fashion designers competing against each other to create the best clothes. In 2012, it entered its tenth season airing on *Lifetime.*

Project Runway is a content brand. Its success has attracted brand partners such as Neiman Marcus (which carries the winning designer's clothes), L'Oreal (which awards a cash prize), *Marie Claire* magazine (which contributes a feature spread in the magazine), and even Hewlett-Packard (which hooks up the winner with $50,000 in technology to run his or her business).

Project Runway is a formidable brandscape and a powerful content brand. The show's format is so successful that it's been transplanted, using what's called a "show bible," to 19 other countries. (You might have a brand style guide at your company that explains how to correctly use your brand. A "show bible" is essentially the brand guidelines for a TV show.)

In June 2011, Jewelers' Circular Keystone (JCK) launched an online video series similar to *Project Runway* called *JCK Rock Star,* featuring five jewelry designers competing against each other to create the most beautiful piece of jewelry. It has all the drama, stress, and conflict of *Project Runway,* but focuses on attracting an entirely different niche audience.

JCK produced 12 webisodes and released them monthly over the course of a year. The winner, Walter Adler Chefitz, was announced in June 2012. The show was incredibly successful for all involved and a second season is in the works.

JCK publishes a magazine, hosts the world's largest jewelry trade show, and creates and distributes content at JCKOnline.com. All of its content is geared toward jewelry industry insiders, people who run retail stores, buy merchandise, and design jewelry. But *JCK Rock Star* doesn't feel that way. It's produced so well that anyone can enjoy it. But if you're in the jewelry business, as most of the audience is, the content takes on a whole new dimension.

JCK doesn't produce the show on its own. Swarovski, the Austrian company that sells luxury jewelry and signature-cut gemstones, underwrites the show and has a judge on the panel of each episode. In addition, each design challenge requires the contestants to incorporate a signature gemstone from the Swarovski collection. (The work these designers create, by the way, is pretty spectacular and creative.) London Jewelers is another partner, representing the retail side of the house.

JCK didn't have to come up with a new content idea. They leveraged an existing concept pioneered by *Project Runway*, skewed the content to make sure it was relevant to their audience, and branded it as a valuable program. Swarovski and London Jewelers pooled their professional expertise and financial resources to make the show a reality. The content is authentic, the brandscape is effective, and the content has built a brand of its own.

Think Like a TV Exec

JCK created a successful content brand because they thought more like television executives than publishers or traditional marketers.

It doesn't matter if you're trying to maintain a blog, design a compelling Twitter strategy, record a podcast, or build a YouTube channel—you'll be far more successful creating a content brand if you think about building a television show.

When I worked in the entertainment business, everyone I met told me they had an idea for a television show. The reality is, in a fragmented marketplace where brands need content to drive meaningful relationships, your idea truly may be the next big thing.

Successful television content is format driven. It follows a formula for each and every episode. While the substance of the content may change, the formula stays the same. This formula (not any piece of content itself) is what the audience builds a relationship with, week in and week out.

Unfortunately, I don't believe there are any "new" formats out there. Neither do television executives. Instead of taking gambles with new content concepts you think might be revolutionary, look for inspiration in the content you already consume.

As a marketer, this should feel liberating. All you have to do is find a successful existing format and emulate it. Just as JCK leveraged the format *Project Runway* pioneered a decade ago, you too can tailor any format to your audience.

To leverage an existing format, you need to think about two important things. First, who is your talent? What personalities can carry the content forward? Second, you need a hook. How are you going to twist the content to work for your audience? How can you ensure it's relevant?

JCK Rock Star didn't need to be a video program. The same content could have been executed as a weekly feature on its website with text and photography. Here's an easy format (in text form) that's easy to emulate—just to illustrate what I'm getting at.

Lifehacker promotes its content as "tips, tricks, and downloads for getting things done." I like their content and I have a weekly relationship with a format they've branded *Hive Five*. Here's how Lifehacker describes *Hive Five*:

> *"The* Hive Five *feature series asks readers to answer the most frequently asked question we get: 'Which tool is the best?' Once a week we'll put out a call for contenders looking for the best solution to a certain problem, then YOU tell us your favorite tools to get the job done. Every weekend, we'll report back with the top five recommendations and give you a chance to vote on which is best."*

There you have it: a format they deliver on week in and week out. I know what to expect, it's valuable to me, and when I see *Hive Five* in my inbox or on my e-reader I dive right in. They've covered everything from the five best weather websites to the most popular productivity method. They've introduced me to the best Bluetooth headset and movie recommendation sites. I get a lot out of this simple format.

Think about what format you can emulate. What topics would the *Hive Five* for your business or industry focus on, and who would cover those subjects?

To develop content that's valuable enough that your audience will want to build a relationship with it, you will have to push the boundaries to find something you can own, something that's worth branding, something that's repeatable.

That's the value of a format. It gives you something you can brand, creates content you can own, and builds a relationship with your viewers, listeners, or readers.

WHAT IF...

Myles Bristowe thinks like a television executive. He doesn't have a television show or even a regularly scheduled video program on YouTube. But he does have a content brand—he's the "marketing cookie guy."

Myles is the CMO of CommCreative and the president of the Boston chapter of the American Marketing Association. But I didn't know any of that before I built a relationship with his content brand. Let me explain.

Every weekday, Myles posts an article branded as "Today's Marketing Cookie" on his company's blog. People from around the world send him photos of fortunes they find in fortune cookies. Each day, Myles reflects on a fortune, connecting it with marketing. He also includes a picture and brief bio of the person who submitted the fortune that he's reflecting on (a perfect example of using brandscaping to leverage the audiences of others).

Myles has set himself up with a simple challenge and it works. I know exactly what to expect every time I receive his weekly recap: five intelligent blog posts that leverage fortune cookie aphorisms to teach me a marketing lesson.

I've recommended Myles' content to other marketing professionals because it's so easy to understand. His content brand is easy to share. It's intriguing and interesting. It's a twist on the all-too-familiar and inconsistent marketing advice you get on other corporate blogs. Myles leverages his content brand to elevate his advice above the noise of commodity content.

What if *you* turned a fortune into a relevant lesson for your audience every day? What would those lessons look like?

Ask Yourself...

How can we package and present our audience with a content brand they can build a relationship with?

In Chapter 7, I asked you to set some expectations for your opt-in audience. It's time to brand those expectations. I know, you're probably trying to brand your product offering already, and now I'm asking you to brand your content. Well, yes. That's how successful content brands are built.

Treat your content like a product. Build a logo for it, as if it were a successful television show. That's exactly what SAY Media has done with its Friday Venn diagrams. It's what Dave Pell has done with his NextDraft daily email featuring fascinating news articles. It's what JCK has done with *JCK Rock Star.*

If you're going to be successful growing an audience for your content, you too will have to brand it like a product. If your content was a brand, what would it look like?

Chapter 15
Reworking the Media

The Media Evolution

Thinking like a television executive and branding your content opens up terrific possibilities to extend the reach of what you create by adding traditional media partners to your brandscape. If your content is good enough, branded well enough, and you can attract an audience, then it's valuable content—content that magazines, digital publishers, television networks, and even radio stations will want to be a part of.

The more brandscaping you do, the more the media sees you as a threat to their business—your efforts siphon money away from their traditional advertising revenue and fragment their audience. That's why smart publishers, like *DC Velocity* and *JCK*, are developing content brands that have the potential to transcend their platforms. Both *Move it!* and *JCK Rock Star* are great content brands built by intelligent media companies that understand the power of deeper relationships with the brands they serve. Successful publishers are moving away from the simple sale of ad time or space, and generating editorial content that moves the market for their sponsors.

Instead of looking to buy ads in the context of an existing program or magazine, brands are beginning to push for a deeper kind of content integration. These brands don't want a relationship that destroys the editorial viability and trust with the audience the media has created—they want to enhance it. They want the media to create content that's more niche focused—more targeted at things they know the audience wants to hear.

Progressive brands don't want infomercials or advertorials. They want to be part of a content brand in ways that look more like public broadcasting (think NPR and PBS), rather than traditional advertising.

The Story of Us

Even big media companies are brandscaping. In 2010, *The History Channel* partnered with Bank of America to produce a six-part, 12-hour miniseries called *America: The Story of Us.* (At the time, *The History Channel* was a trusted source for historical documentaries, rather than the programming it's airing today with shows like *Swamp People* and *American Pickers*.)

In the midst of the economic downturn's slow recovery, *The Story of Us* focused on the country's ability to capitalize on opportunities, no matter what obstacles, by pursuing innovation and big thinking. It showcased how the Erie Canal brought risks, but big rewards. It covered the Civil War by focusing on the Union's ability to leverage technology to win. It highlighted the ability of the transcontinental railroad to transform the American Heartland. The series was unbelievably inspiring, interesting, and compelling.

The stories were well told and the caliber of the commentary was phenomenal. Episodes included interviews with everyone from Olympic athlete Bruce Jenner to astronaut Buzz Aldrin. Other big names included Sean "Diddy" Combs, Newt Gingrich, Bill Maher, and even President Obama. It was a superstar affair. (As a side note, that's a brandscape.)

Now remember, at the time the series aired, the global financial crisis and the economic downturn had left the general public skeptical, frustrated, and even fearful that the economy may never fully recover. In the eyes of millions of Americans, Bank of America was part of the mortgage meltdown that precipitated the problem. The bank had recently took out a $45 billion loan from the American public, and perception of the brand wasn't good.

"We recognize that a lot of consumers are distrustful and skeptical of banks right now," Meredith Verdone, Bank of America's senior vice president for brand advertising, told the *Los Angeles Times*.[21]

But instead of waiting for the crisis to blow over, Bank of America decided to do something about it. That's part of why it decided to get involved in *The Story of Us*. This was, however, no ordinary "ad buy."

Instead of running 30-second commercials during the program, Bank of America asked *History* to produce a series of inspirational and emotional two-minute mini-documentaries. The "ads" (if you can call them that) integrated seamlessly into the flow of the program.

For example, in an early episode highlighting the American colonists eager to rise up against the British, the Bank of America mini-documentary tells the story of the financial problems they faced. "The British used money as a way of keeping the Americans down," says a historian. "The British controlled the money supply. There were no banks." Then the narrator chimes in, "On July 5, 1784, The Massachusetts Bank opens for business. Today, it has grown with our nation to become Bank of America."

The "ad" goes on to remind us that Paul Revere and John Hancock were customers of that very first bank. It feels like part of the series, sounds like part of the series, and even includes the same interview subjects from the show.

In a similar spot, following the segment about the Erie Canal, the Bank of America mini-doc shows how one of the banks that funded the canal is now part of Bank of America.

With each mini-documentary, Bank of America tied its history into *The Story of Us*. They even took it a step further to show us how they're still contributing to innovation and expansion in America.

"When *The History Channel* came to us with this opportunity, it was a neat fit because we are inextricably linked to pivotal points in U.S. history," Meredith Verdone also said. "Our legacy as a company is that we have always fueled opportunity."[22]

The content was compelling. The show was well-produced. But, did it work? Did *The History Channel* get the ratings it needed? Did Bank of America help change the way the public saw its brand?

New Media Relations

America: The Story of Us became the most-watched special in *The History Channel's* history. The first episode alone had 5.7 million viewers. In addition, Bank of America's sponsorship (approximately $5 million) was the largest single transaction for *The History Channel* that year.

In a brandscaping world, a brand like Bank of America, which serves about 20 million customers, is a powerful audience generation engine. During the weeks leading up to the premiere of the series, Bank of America promoted the program on its website and on video monitors in more than 1,000 banks. The bank also got a tremendous amount of press coverage for its partnership with *History* in publications such as *The New York Times* and *Businessweek*, reaching an additional 9.8 million people.

When *The Story of Us* ended, Bank of America saw incredible "brand perception gains." Trustworthiness of the bank was up 42 percent. Favorability of the brand skyrocketed up 50 percent. Amazingly, consideration of the bank as a service provider was up 54 percent.[23]

Through the tremendous amount of press coverage the bank generated, Bank of America had successfully leveraged a brandscape partnership to inspire Americans to look past the financial crisis. It also helped Americans look to the Bank of America brand as a trusted partner in rebuilding the American economy.

Were the mini-docs more successful than running traditional ads? The audience reported that the spots were 57 percent more effective and 29 percent more emotional than other advertisements. Ninety-six percent of the audience watched every spot.[24]

Bank of America could not have been as successful in changing the public's opinion with a press release or a traditional ad buy. It took a deep partnership with *The History Channel* that leveraged both audiences. It took a brandscape between a banking behemoth and a broadcast network.

Doesn't this new media model look more like one pioneered by public broadcasting 50 years ago—one that focuses on underwriting instead of advertising? Does this remind you of Irna Phillips and her soap operas?

If you're already spending money on ads in a trade magazine or on a website, it's time to rethink your relationships with your media partners. Encourage them to tell stories that will raise demand and interest in the products you sell. Have them cover issues your customers face on a daily basis. Require that they get more targeted and less general. Ask them how you can help them succeed in creating content your audience will consume. Be more like a Bank of America, and think more like an underwriter than an advertiser.

Keep this in mind: Just because you no longer have to work with the media, it doesn't mean you don't need the media. Media brands are really proficient at maintaining a loyal audience and creating great content. They have all the earmarks of a good brandscaping partner. You just need to start asking them the right questions and pushing them to add more value beyond display advertising.

WHAT IF...

America: The Story of Us was a six-week affair. As far as I know, that was the end of the brandscape partnership between Bank of America and *The History Channel*, which seems sad to me. If the end result was so successful for both brands, why wouldn't they explore ways to extend the relationship?

The $5 million Bank of America spent on this project was a drop in the bucket when you consider the size of its annual advertising spend of $464 million in 2010.

What if the bank had pledged to underwrite a weekly show that dove in even deeper to the history of innovation in our country? Let's imagine the series had a budget of $10 million. That would be huge for *The History Channel,* but still just a small percentage of the bank's total annual spend.

With a weekly show, Bank of America could continue to remind Americans how financial institutions like theirs have lead to the success of companies like Ford Motor Company and AT&T. Where would we be without the automobile and the phone? Or we could hear stories of how Hewlett-Packard got started in a garage and how Texas Instruments invented the integrated circuit. *The Story of Us* isn't just 400 years over six nights. There are at least 10 seasons of content there.

If six episodes proved to be so successful in raising awareness and positive brand favorability, what if Bank Of America invested in more content, more often, by leveraging their *History* relationship?

What if you worked with a trade publication, magazine or digital publisher to make an impact on your business?

Ask Yourself...

Can we find a better way to pay for the creation of the content our audience wants from the media brands they trust?

Before you start creating and branding content (like a new product), it makes sense to step back and decide whether your existing media partners (the people you may already advertise with) might be interested in doing this with you.

The fact is, those trade magazines, digital content publishers, and even television networks don't want to lose your valuable advertising dollars. Don't cut them off without asking them if they'd put your money to more effective use. Let's face it: they're really good at creating content your audience already engages with. They have an audience that trusts their editorial insight. All you have to do is ask them to spend your money more like Bank of America spent theirs—on creating content that's relevant to your audience.

Sure, you'll buy advertising (if that's what they want to call it), but only if they start creating the kind of content that has an effect on the market. Otherwise, you're better off investing those dollars elsewhere.

Are your media partners really *partners*—or are they just interested in the dollars you spend?

Chapter 16
From Twitter to TV

The Channel as a Media Brand

Working with the media is one way to help you build a brandscape with reach. But the media charges you for access to their audience. In a Galilean universe, you should also be treating channels like YouTube, Flickr, Tumblr, Twitter, and Facebook as media channels—media channels where accessing a massive audience is free.

I don't need to dole out a long list of stats to prove these channels have an audience. You already know that. You're more interested in learning how to capitalize on those audiences to drive revenue.

Instead of thinking of a channel like YouTube as a pipe delivering disparate content to your audience, think of it as a cable provider like Comcast or Verizon. YouTube is a content hub. Instead of using a remote to change channels with scheduled programming (like you do with traditional cable), you're the programming director and there's more than just an up or down button. YouTube is an a la carte cable provider. You pick and choose from programming you want to watch, when you want to watch it. Hulu, Amazon, and Netflix are no different. Neither is Twitter.

On Twitter, instead of cable TV channels, there are hashtags. Hashtags let you filter out content that's irrelevant to you. For example, if I'm interested in a conference called *Content Marketing World*, and its hashtag is #CMWorld, I can tune into everything that's going on at *Content Marketing World* by only "watching" the #CMWorld channel.

When you think like a television executive and build programming on social media channels, you can attract an unbelievably targeted and engaged audience. That's exactly what Justin Halpern did to build a massive following on Twitter.

$#*! My Dad Says

In 2009, at age 29, Justin Halpern moved back in with his parents in San Diego. At the time, he was a writer for *Maxim* magazine and had all but given up on his dream of being a screenwriter in Hollywood. For years, Justin had kept a journal of the funny, and often foul-mouthed, life lessons his father imparted in everyday conversations. Now that he was living at home, Justin heard new ones every day.

At the suggestion of a friend, Justin joined Twitter on August 3, 2009, using the handle @ShitMyDadSays and he started publishing his father's musings as Twitter status updates on a regular basis. (Warning: a lot of the stuff Justin's dad says is profane.) Here are a few tweets that capture the essence of his dad's advice:

"No. Aliens exist, I just don't think they came millions of light years just to see Earth. Be like driving 1,000 miles to go to an Arby's."

"I didn't say you were ugly. I said your girlfriend is better looking than you, and standing next to her, you look ugly."

Justin's tweet stream was supposed to be a place for Justin to store his dad's "rhetorical gems." But within a few weeks, the quotes had garnered him 100,000 followers. The audience was so valuable—and the content so focused, interesting, and funny—that by October 2009, Harper Collins, one of the world's largest publishing companies, had signed a book deal with Justin.

A month later, Justin's Twitter following had reached 1.8 million, just as he signed a television deal with Warner Bros. In March 2010, a sitcom, called *$#*! My Dad Says* (pronounced bleep my dad says), started shooting, and by May, CBS picked up the show. That very same month, Justin's book hit Amazon and bookstores around the nation. By June, the book topped *The New York Times* Best Seller list for hardcover nonfiction.

In less than a year, Justin had gone from a down-and-out screenwriter-wannabe to a best-selling author, screenwriter, and sitcom producer, and it all started by building a valuable audience on Twitter. Today, his audience is still growing. At last check, he had slightly more than 3 million followers.

You Have to Start Somewhere

I know from listening to numerous interviews with Justin, that he had no deep strategy for building a successful career on Twitter. But as a media strategist and marketing professional, I think he happened upon a really smart approach to building his brand. There are three reasons Justin's strategy was so successful.

First, he thinks like a television executive. Justin actually tweets his dad's quotes pretty infrequently, but his format never waivers. He doesn't tweet what he ate for breakfast. He doesn't even interact with his followers (he only follows one person, and that's Levar Burton). He's never clouded his content and he stays true to the expectation he set for his audience. In fact, his Twitter profile sets everyone up for what he's going to deliver: "I'm 29. I live with my 74-year-old dad. He is awesome. I just write down shit that he says."

Second, he's built a content brand. Whether he knew it or not when he set out to store his dad's sayings on Twitter, Justin created a brand—a brand so powerful that Harper Collins wanted a part of it. A brand so well-executed CBS figured out a way to make it broadcast friendly. Justin never imagined the brand would be that smart, but I have to think that all his work pitching screenplays in Los Angeles helped position his content in a way that captured people's attention.

Third, he started small and stayed focused on one channel to build an audience. He didn't have to write an entire screenplay or a novel—all he had to do was cut to the chase. He gave you the punchline without the rest of the joke. There was obviously more to it, or he wouldn't have been able to write a best-selling book. Justin didn't have a "Facebook strategy." He didn't have a YouTube channel and a LinkedIn group. He didn't even bother with a blog that was worth reading (Justin did have a blog, but it seems like something his publisher forced him to do).

You don't need a giant video strategy or a massive budget to think like a television executive. You don't have to hire a creative agency to build a content brand and fashion a campaign around it. You don't have to do everything big when you have access to an audience. You just have to be good.

Go ahead, start a new Twitter handle right now. Deliver just one piece of good content on it every single day. Let your coworkers, business partners, and customers know you're doing it and see if you can't start small. If you don't believe it can work, check out Clients From Hell @ClientsFH on Twitter (http://twitter.com/#!/clientsfh).

WHAT IF…

Justin Halpern's television sitcom on CBS was a failure. It was canceled after only one season, even though (or maybe because) it starred William Shatner. I watched a couple of episodes, and I'll be honest, it wasn't very good. Justin wanted a television show. It was his dream. But what if Justin had turned down CBS? Did he really need them?

What if Justin had actually learned from the success he had on Twitter and translated it into a YouTube channel? Don't you think his audience would have followed him to watch uncensored content there? Content that was more true to his brand and his father's unique comedy? If only 25 percent of Justin's Twitter audience came to watch his content on YouTube, that would be 750,000 weekly viewers. Sure, that's less than the 10 million viewers CBS generated for the show, but I'd imagine Justin could have grown his audience on YouTube the same way he did on Twitter. There are channels on YouTube with 5 million subscribers. That's a powerhouse in the digital world.

What if Justin would have rethought his dream of writing and producing a traditional TV sitcom? Would he have an audience if he'd produced the show for YouTube? I'd bet on it.

You don't need a network to produce a television show. You don't need a publisher to print a book. You don't need a radio station to create a podcast. You can take advantage of the changes in distribution to bypass traditional media and build an audience on your own.

Ask Yourself...

How can we experiment with our content brand without investing too much, too fast?

In Chapter 8, I asked you to identify one channel, closer to the center of your target audience's universe, where you could focus your energy. Maybe it's YouTube, Twitter, or LinkedIn. It doesn't matter. What you need to do is take the expectations you've set for your audience and the content brand you'd like to build and start experimenting rapidly on that channel.

Let's say your audience is participating in a LinkedIn group. You've set the expectation that every week you're going to distribute a relevant industry chart that will help them with their business. Let's assume you've branded it as "Steal this Slide." (Isn't that already more exciting?)

You don't have to set up a new website, start a blog, or create a video. All you have to do is post it every week on LinkedIn to see if it resonates with your audience. I guarantee that within a few weeks, you'll know if you're adding value. If it's successful, go for it, expand the brand. Start creating "Steal This Slide" videos that help explain the chart.

It's really difficult, no matter how big or small you are, to be successful on every new media channel. What channel can you start small on, knowing that your idea might grow into something big?

Part Three
Content is Currency

A good brandscaper looks at content as a form of currency. It's something that can be used as a medium of exchange. Ford Motor Company obviously found Ken Block's Gymkhana series valuable enough to invest in it. Sephora obviously saw value in Lauren Luke's content. The software company Awareness has leveraged valuable content from authors to fuel its brand power.

It's entirely possible that the future of all media is branded. I can imagine a world where TV commercials don't exist—where magazines are advertising-free. Instead, the content is underwritten by brands that understand the power and value of the content they create, own, share, and trade. (This is the single-greatest threat to today's media companies, but that's a topic for another book.)

Once you shift your focus away from paying for access to an audience to one that views content as an asset, you will see a dramatic transformation in your business.

Chapter 17
Your Content is Valuable

Content Has Legs

Content is a form of intellectual capital; unlike an advertising buy, it's something you own. It's something you can repackage, resell, and redistribute. It's something you can promote, share, discuss, trade, and debate with a valuable set of existing and likely consumers. Content is around forever—an advertising buy is not.

In a digital era defined by an insatiable demand for content, you need content to remain top-of-mind and to keep your target audience engaged. There is no one in the marketing universe who believes they can ever have enough high-quality, relevant content to share with their audience. They certainly can't keep up if they're going to attempt to create it on their own.

There are wonderful stories of bloggers turning into bestsellers (*Stuff White People Like*), tweets turning into television shows (*$#*! My Dad Says*), Academy Award-nominated films being produced by brands (*Food, Inc.* and *Stonyfield Farm*), even jingles turning into number-one singles (Chris Brown's commercial for Wrigley Gum).

A good brandscaper strives to create content that is inherently valuable—the kind of content that traditional media outlets (TV networks, magazines, radio stations) could sell advertising against. If your content is *that* valuable it becomes a revenue opportunity—an asset instead of an expense.

Beer Anyone?

Have you ever heard of or watched the show *Brew Masters*? *Discovery Channel* used to air it on Sunday nights. The star of the show was Sam Calagione, the founder and CEO of Dogfish Head Craft Brewery. Sam had written (or co-authored) three books and produced a series of "Dogfish-inspired" short films. *Discovery Channel* talent scouts "discovered" him while watching his YouTube videos.

Each episode of *Brew Masters* followed Sam and his team as they traveled around the world looking for new, ancient, or imaginative inspiration for beer.

"They [Discovery Channel] could see we take beer very seriously, but we don't take ourselves too seriously," Sam explained in a *Wall Street Journal* interview. They thought it would be great to "see the world of beer and how exciting it is through the eyes of one little company."[25]

The content was compelling. In one episode, Sam and his team traveled to Peru to make a beer fermented from chewed corn and saliva. In another, they traveled to Egypt to find ancient spices for a new brew. In yet another, Sam brandscaped with Sony Records to celebrate the 40th anniversary of Miles Davis' album, *Bitches Brew*. The challenge: brew and ship 50,000 bottles before the anniversary deadline.

Having a show on *Discovery Channel* made a huge impact on Sam's business. Brand interest in Dogfish Head doubled in October 2010 when *Brew Masters* debuted. By December, after five episodes had aired, Dogfish Head's online brand value increased another 50 percent.[26]

Unfortunately, *Brew Masters* was not renewed. Rumor has it that it was canceled because "big beer" threatened to pull its advertising from the network if the show was continued.[27]

Now, think about this—Dogfish Head's content, internal talent, and approach was so valuable that a television network created a show focused around it, and then sold air time to other brands that couldn't find an authentic, engaging, and exciting story to tell.

Did the content itself impact Dogfish Head's sales? You bet it did.

"After *Discovery* aired an episode about Dogfish Head's new imperial stout, Bitches Brew, there was a run on liquor stores, and the beer—which retails for around $15 per 22-ounce bottle—quickly sold out," according to an article that appeared in the *Boston Globe*.[28]

Even though *Brew Masters* was cancelled, do you really think Sam Calagione "needs" *Discovery*? What if he just went back to YouTube?

Imagine if Sam and his team brandscaped with one partner every month, split the production costs to film brewing-related adventures, and shared the episodes online? *Discovery* proved Sam's content was valuable—all he really needs to do now is tap into the intrinsic and inherent value of his content.

Content Takes on a Life of its Own

If your content is valuable enough to be re-sold by a television network, published in a magazine, referenced on someone else's blog, or even shared on Facebook, it's an asset. It's got value.

If you're constantly creating digital assets as advertisements and promotions, they have no value. They're just expenses—expenses that force you to measure the ROI to justify the expense. If you're constantly sending promotions, discounts, and self-affirming crap, you aren't building your brand or providing your audience with valuable content—you're bribing them to open your email, or asking them to take advantage of an offer. Most of the time, they're probably just deleting your messages.

Is your content intrinsically valuable? If it's not, stop creating it and start over. Stop thinking of your content as a campaign or a marketing expense, and start investing in it as intellectual property. Think of it as something you can own. Treat it like an asset, not an expense.

WHAT IF...

Brandscaping has the power to reinvent the way traditional television networks find and build their programming. But, it also has the power to revolutionize entire industries. Ben Kaufman did both by the time he turned 25.

In 2009, Ben set up a booth at a tech industry trade show called Macworld. Although he'd invented a set of retractable headphones, he needed a new product to market—a new concept. So, Ben invited conference attendees to submit their ideas for new iPhone accessories. Over the course of two days, he amassed 100 inventions captured as sketches and clipped them to a clothesline in his booth. Each idea was uploaded to the web and he invited his social media audience to rate and rank each idea. By the third day of the conference, Ben began prototyping what would become his new product line.

Ben loved the collaborative process of creating a new product so much that he sold his headphone company and immediately started a new one called Quirky. Quirky leverages everyone's ideas to create new products in a process Ben calls "open-source invention and product development."

Traditional product design is a long, slow process leveraging tons of market research and design experimentation to arrive at a successful new product launch. Quirky leverages its online audience of 221,000 people to get a product into stores in three months. (Remember, every single one of those people has his or her own audience.)

Here's how it works. Quirky users can submit an idea to the Quirky community. The audience votes on each idea with the best and most popular ones bubbling to the top. The company's team of design and development experts picks two ideas a week to bring to market. When the products hit store shelves at brandscape partners like Target, Bed Bath & Beyond, Barnes and Noble, Toys-R-Us, and Staples (to name a few), the originator of the idea receives 35 percent of the revenue.

Everyone wins! The inventor of one of Quirky's first products, called Pivot Power (an adjustable power strip that holds large adapters in every outlet), was a student at the Rhode Island School of Design when he submitted his first idea. To date, he's earned nearly $300,000 in royalties. Quirky has revolutionized the entire product design industry. Ben's a brandscaping whiz.

Quirky's process, in the early days, was so transparent that they created a YouTube channel to broadcast their creative process and even interview the originators of each chosen idea. They'd listen to the highest-ranked pitches as a team and challenge the inventors to justify the consumer demand. It was really compelling content that drove interest in the products they were vetting, but also in the drama behind the design process.

Quirky's content was so valuable, so entertaining, that a television network turned it into a reality show. *Quirky* aired for the first time in August 2011 on the *Sundance* channel.

So, while *Brew Masters* went straight to television and should consider going back to YouTube, Quirky started on YouTube and graduated to TV.

Ben Kaufman hasn't just revolutionized the process of bringing a product to market and building an audience or his content, he's revolutionized the way television networks find and secure new content—content that already attracts hundreds of thousands of online viewers.

What if you started showing your work in an entertaining and exciting way, like Quirky? What if you found yourself featuring your business on national TV?

Ask Yourself...

Are we treating our content as an asset, or an expense?

I don't want you contributing to information overload, and I don't want you wasting money on futile marketing efforts that don't drive demand. That's why I asked you in Chapter 6 to make a list of things you should stop doing.

Look back at that list. How many of those things could be considered intellectual property—an asset? Coupon codes and promotions don't count. Neither do contests, offers, or link-laden corporate news updates. Webinars do—if they're so good that other brands want to be a part of them. Ditto for blogs.

Your content's not worth anything unless someone else thinks it is. Start building a budget for your new brandscaping adventures by crossing off the things that don't add value to your company's bottom line, and focusing on the things that do.

Chapter 18
Frequency, Quality, Relevance

Who Determines Value?

In the digital world, the value of your content is determined by the audience it garners on a regular basis.

Content that gets a million views on YouTube is probably great content, but it's not necessarily valuable. A channel on YouTube with a million subscribers *is* valuable. Why? Because a subscriber makes a commitment to consume the content you're creating. Remember, we live in an opt-in world.

To get people to commit to your content, it has to be relevant to them—and you have to deliver it frequently. It also has to be of high quality—and I'm talking quality in terms of substance, not necessarily production value.

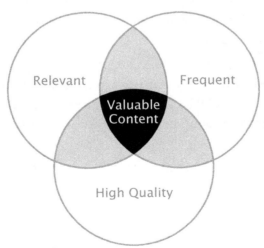

VIRTUES OF VALUABLE CONTENT

Figure 4: Valuable content is found at the intersection of frequency, quality, and relevance.

How Frequency Factors In

I only know of one company that delivers one piece of content a day that's built a truly formidable brand—that brand is TED.

TED stands for Technology, Entertainment, Design. TED holds two annual conferences (one in Long Beach, California, and one in Edinburg, Scotland), plus the brand has grown to include a TEDIndia conference, a TEDWomen conference, and a local franchise-style conference called TEDx.

Each conference features invited speakers from around the world. The goal is to "share ideas worth spreading." The speakers represent a wide range of topics across research, science, culture, and art. Each speaker has 18 minutes (max) to present his or her inspiring ideas on stage and they're captured on video.

The TED conferences generate tons of content, but the organizers release only one quality video per day. These "TEDTalks," as they're branded, have been viewed by more than 500 million people around the world. (If you've never watched a TED Talk you're in for a treat. Take a look at TED.com or subscribe to their YouTube channel. You're bound to be inspired.)

TED's audience is valuable. So valuable, in fact, that the organizers have been able to sell sponsorship opportunities for the videos they release. Brands like BMW, Tiffany & Co., Rolex, and IBM have all spent considerable amounts of money to attach themselves to TED's inspired thinking.

Delivering well-formatted content with consistent frequency builds relationships. Relationships build trust. Trust drives revenue. TED has mastered—and monetized—this idea.

But do you have to deliver content *every* day? No—but TED is proof you can. If you do choose to deliver content every day, make sure it's valuable. Spitting out random thoughts on your blog every morning is not going to help you build valuable relationships with a committed audience. Quality content will.

What Constitutes Quality?

Let's face it—PowerPoint presentations are boring. TED Talks are not. Most conferences I attend have really poor presenters and low production values. TED events do not. Some TED presenters rehearse for months to prepare for their 18 minutes on stage. TED presenters are polished, they tell phenomenal stories, they drive emotion, and they command the audience's attention. TED is the Super Bowl of presentations.

TED values quality over quantity. Could the TED organizers find 50 presentation videos to share every day? Sure they could. But they don't.

In a world where the barriers to creating content have dropped so low, high-quality content is a commodity that attracts audiences. But what constitutes quality? It depends on your business and the type of content that's already available in your market. If you're in the conference business, TED has raised the bar. Put on a TED-like event and you'll pack the house. Produce and share TED-quality conference videos and you'll drive attendance.

I'm not saying that you have to have slick production. But you do need to understand what your audience is already consuming. What defines "high quality" for *your* target market, given what you already see? Can you do better? If so, you have an opportunity.

Take Lauren Luke for example. At the time she released her first makeup tutorial, none of the major makeup brands were doing how-to videos for teenagers on YouTube. Lauren had no competition and her message was authentic. She put out high-quality content that had low production value. In fact, she was so shy in her first video that she didn't even speak. It didn't matter. Her tutorial was better than anything else out there. She'd found an opportunity to create content that no one else had pursued, and she owned it.

How Relevance Impacts Authority

TED Talks cover an unbelievably wide array of issues and topics. But they all feature one thing in common: inspiring ideas.

TED Talks aren't relevant to the audience simply because of the subject matter they cover, but because of the emotion they impart. You can't help but feel stirred after watching a presentation about sustainable packaging in which an innovative, young entrepreneur demonstrates how he can grow packaging material from fungi.

Creating relevant content for your audience doesn't have to focus on inspired ideas. Nevertheless, if you wrote a blog post last week about your Super Bowl picks or how much your cat likes milk with the hopes of being relevant to your B2B customers, you've completely missed the mark.

When you deliver content that's irrelevant to your audience—either because you don't understand their wants and needs or because you're not putting forth the proper effort—you diminish your authority in your industry.

On the other hand, relevant content—delivered at a "high enough" quality—on a frequent basis, creates a valuable asset. But that's not enough. You have to build a format, too.

WHAT IF...

Conferences, trade shows, expositions, and seminars are the most underutilized content creation opportunities for brands of every industry and size. Every event is a brandscape in-and-of-itself: a series of brands have come together to target the very same audience.

These real-world events are packed with industry experts, luminaries, and successful brands, all eager to tell their story and expand their reach.

What if you leveraged one event per year by investing in the creation of some high-quality, relevant content for your audience? What if you interviewed 52 industry experts about a single, simple topic or theme over the course of four days, and then distributed one interview per week over the next 52 weeks? You'd have a year's worth of content and a series guaranteed to attract audience interest.

What if you took it a step further and actually partnered with TED to create a TED-branded event for your own industry? What if you brandscaped with one of the most prolific conference brands in the world?

Ask Yourself...

How do we identify what content is valuable to our audience?

In Chapter 2, I asked you to make a list of the content your audience is already consuming. Rank that content (on a scale of 1-10) for each of the three virtues of valuable content: Is it frequently delivered? Is it high-quality? Is it relevant to *your* brand?

The higher the mark that any one piece of content gets, the more valuable it is to you and your audience. Who's creating that content? These are the people and brands you want to brandscape with. These are the partners you want to build real-world relationships with.

Chapter 19
Build a Format

The Formula for Creating an Asset

Format is the way you structure, organize, and present content. The format (not the content itself) is what an audience builds a relationship with—it's what they get comfortable with. Some of the most valuable content on the web is that which follows a specific format. A consistent format delivers a consistent audience.

Creating a format for your content is essential. While the substance might change from week-to-week or month-to-month, the content format shouldn't. Formatting content isn't just for video. It works with any type of media. A good podcast has a format. My favorite blogs deliver formatted content. Even my bank sends a formatted statement each month. (I don't like my bank statement but I have built a relationship with it.)

A Lesson from *The A-Team*

Television programs are notoriously well-formatted content. While a program's talent helps make a show successful, it's actually the format that defines the show's long-term staying power. Formats ensure that the writers stick to the same program elements that keep viewers coming back week-in and week-out. Formats guarantee that viewers won't be surprised by content they didn't expect or don't like. Formats dictate the recipe for any successful show.

If you were of age in the 1980s, you might remember a prime-time program called *The A-Team*. As a child of that decade, I watched every episode featuring the "heroes for hire." The premise of the show was simple: four Vietnam vets, framed for a crime they didn't commit, help the innocent while on the run from the military. Every episode followed a very simple format.

The show opened by identifying someone in need of assistance—a person who couldn't go to the local authorities for some reason or another. Enter The A-Team who would devise a plan to scare off the villains. The episode would climax with a music montage during which the heroes fought back the bad guys. Meanwhile the military, in pursuit of The A-Team, would come close to capturing the team of misfits, but The A-Team would survive on the run for another day. At the end of every episode, their situation was exactly the same as when the episode started. This simple format kept the show running for four years.

Have you heard the phrase "jumped the shark"? In the television business, a show is said to have "jumped the shark" when the "quality" has declined beyond recovery. The phrase owes its genesis to a particularly farcical episode of *Happy Days* when the show's main character, Fonzie, literally jumped a shark on a trip to Hollywood. As soon as a show strays from its format, it's destined to "jump the shark."

The A-Team's pivotal shark-jumping moment came in season five, when the team was captured by the military, a direct deviation from the show's recipe for success. Seven episodes later, the show was canceled.

Audiences love a format. No matter what medium you select—be it text, audio, imagery, or video—distributing content that follows a strict format greatly increases your chances for success.

In the digital world, it's no different. You need a format if you're going to capture the consistent attention, interest, and eyeballs of your chosen audience.

=3 = 1.6 Billion Views

How has Ray William Johnson—an Oklahoma native living in New York City with no giant media partner—built the most subscribed to YouTube channel today? He has a reliable, consistent format from which he never strays. The audience knows what to expect—and when to expect it.

Ray's show, *=3* (http://www.youtube.com/user/RayWilliamJohnson), has more than 5.3 million subscribers (warning: his content is not family-friendly). Over the last four years, he's garnered 1.6 billion (that's not a typo) video views. An average of 2,500 new people subscribe to Ray's channel every day. Each video he uploads gets almost 2 million video views in the first 48 hours.

Ray started uploading YouTube video commentary twice a week in 2008. Every Tuesday and Friday, he finds three new YouTube videos (hence the show's title =3) and provides his unique blend of video-inspired comedy. He states right at the top of his YouTube channel, "New episodes every Tuesday and Friday." His content follows the formula of "appointment consumption," which we'll talk about in greater detail further on.

The Joe Show, which we talked about earlier in the book, is formatted content, too. Every *Joe Show* is structured the exact same way. The graphics present us with a theme. One week it might be "big and small" and the next week it might be "spring flings." Over the course of the next three to four minutes, Joe Haley reviews five products, and for each one, helps us think about a sales idea that would be effective for our clients. As simple as that is, it's a format.

A Recipe for Your Content

A good format becomes part of your intellectual property. It's something you own and it can transcend the person who writes or records it. Take *American Idol*, for example. The talent has changed, but the format has not.

Commodity content (content that has no format) must rely on constant promotional efforts to grow its audience. One day it's great, the next it's not. Content that's formatted intelligently grows organically—it will be shared by an audience that identifies with it.

Formatted content gets easier and easier to create the more you do it. But creating a winning recipe isn't easy. It takes some trial and error. It takes some time to figure out what works and what doesn't.

WHAT IF...

Deloitte is the second largest professional services consulting firm in the world. Each week, buried on their website, they release a new piece of content that follows a terrific format. It's called *Deloitte Debates*.

Deloitte Debates covers a wide range of topics. Each post begins with an introduction to the issue at hand. Then they outline the debate in a slick graphic format. For each point, there's a counterpoint. Finally, the format closes with an editorial-style opinion, called *My Take*, provided by a Deloitte consultant. It's wonderfully executed and refreshingly concise (for a consulting firm). And most importantly, it's something repeatable that I can build a relationship with.

Each *Deloitte Debate* meets the same expectation they've set, which means it's much more likely I'll subscribe and consume the content each week.

I only have one issue with *Deloitte Debates*. While they've tried to build a content brand, it's not one I'd love to embrace and share as a brandscaper. Instead of branding it as a "Deloitte" debate, couldn't they have found something much more universal? The content is so good that I can actually see a CNBC television version of it. But CNBC isn't going to air a show called *Deloitte Debates*. They may, however, entertain the idea of producing a show called *Point + Counterpoint*.

What if Deloitte was humble enough to invite real business luminaries to weigh in on each episode? What if Deloitte thought really big and imagined something like a CEO game show that might air on CNBC? I'd watch that. What if Deloitte started brandscaping—even with some of their own clients—to create content about issues they want their prospects thinking about?

What if *Deloitte Debates* had a better hook?

Ask Yourself...

What content has successfully garnered our audience's attention in the past?

One of the best ways to hone in on a consistent format for your content is to look at what's worked in the past. Is there a blog post that drove an unusually large amount of traffic? Maybe you released a YouTube video that has been consumed more than the others you've posted?

Try to determine whether it was the format that was successful or the content itself. Break the content down into its core elements. Maybe it started with a two-line introductory sentence hypothesizing about a big problem in the market? Maybe it started with a controversial statement that others in your industry would take offense to? Next, you might have defended that statement or your grand hypothesis with three short paragraphs centered around one accessible example from the marketplace. Then, you wrapped it all up with a big question.

As you unravel the core elements that made up the content (line-by-line, paragraph-by-paragraph), you're actually separating the content from the format. Now all you have to do is use the exact same format (your "recipe") using a different controversial statement or a new hypothesis. If you see the same sort of lift and audience engagement consistently over time, you've got a format that works!

Take your recipe and experiment. Cover different topics using the same format and see what resonates with your audience.

Chapter 20
Hook 'em

Avoiding Commodity Content

If you're going to create valuable content for your target audience, and you're going to stick to a format, you must have a hook. Formats give your content structure—a hook gives it character. A hook is, quite simply, a *unique content concept that's designed to ensnare and trap your unsuspecting audience into consuming and sharing your content.*

Hooks enable your audience to build a relationship with the content each time it's delivered. A twist on a familiar structure is what makes your content unique. A hook is what people talk about.

A boring, two-minute industrial video doesn't have a hook. Every television show you watch has a hook.

Deloitte has a great format for *Deloitte Debates*, but they have no hook. A hook would be turning *Deloitte Debates* into a CEO game show. That's compelling. That's something people would talk about. That's something people would share and want to be a part of (if Deloitte would get over itself and change the content brand).

The web was full of makeup tutorials before Lauren Luke came along, but her hook was *celebrity-inspired* makeup tutorials. There were lots of infomercials for blenders and cooking appliances before *Will It Blend?* Tom Dickson's hook was to blend things *that should never be blended.* Ford Motor Co. could have created their own autocross videos, but instead they partnered with Ken Block to do it bigger and better than anyone else. They themed each Gymkhana video as a spectacle with a theme. That's their hook.

No one's created more extreme sporting content than energy drink manufacturer Red Bull. Red Bull is a great example of a brandscaper. They've sponsored extreme skiing films. They run a nationwide cliff diving tour (and they even stream the content live). They've embraced skateboarding, skydiving, ultra-marathoning, and mountain biking—

and that's just the tip of the iceberg. But their content doesn't have a hook. There are lots of documentary-style people profiles, slick editing and graphics, energetic music, and plenty of Red Bull logos—but there isn't much content branding. Red Bull creates a lot of commodity content. Red Bull is a gigantic brand, and maybe they can afford to create commodity content. You can't. You need a hook.

Red Bull is trying to attract the "extreme audience"—something a guy named Devin Graham does quite well.

The Water Jet Pack & Extreme Music Videos

Devin Graham creates energetic extreme sports music videos. That's how I'd describe his hook. If you think mountain biking is extreme, you haven't seen Devin's "huge bike jump into a pond" music video. Like snowboarding? Maybe you should experiment with saltboarding—that's snowboarding pulled by ATVs on the salt flats in the desert. Like rock climbing? Check out his video about the world's largest rope swing.

Devin releases a new extreme music video every week. He's got frequency down. His production value is phenomenal. The substance of his music videos is consistently good. Quality? Check. His videos speak to a young, hip, male audience. Everything from his music choices to the extreme experiments he shoots appeals greatly to his target audience. Devin's relevant. He's got a format that's working for him—music videos. None of what he does is undeniably unique—except for his hook.

In early 2011, as Devin was getting his YouTube channel up and running, he happened on a mediocre marketing video for an extreme product he knew his audience would love. The product was called the JetLev R200. Essentially, it's a water jet pack you strap on your back allowing you to fly across the water. Instead of propelling you with air, the jet pack has a giant hose that sucks up water and pushes it out the bottom of the jet pack. Imagine something you've seen in a James Bond movie levitating across the water. That's the JetLev. It's extremely awesome.

Devin approached the JetLev team about shooting one of his signature music videos for free. All they had to do was pay for his travel to Florida where the company was based.

"They were skeptical at first," Devin remembers. "They imagined my YouTube channel was just a bunch of kids. The JetLev costs more than $100,000, which is a lot if you're hoping these kids are going to save up their allowance to buy one. I told them that, yes, my videos attract a lot of younger consumers, but those consumers have parents and their parents have money."

JetLev agreed to have Devin come down and create one of his extreme music videos. The end result is spectacular. Go ahead, see for yourself (http://bit.ly/DevinJetLev). Devin manages to capture not only what a JetLev R200 is, but the fun and excitement it generates. Most importantly, he captures the emotional reaction you get from owning one of these flying contraptions.

Within a few weeks, the JetLev extreme music video had been viewed by more than 1 million people. The video attracted a wide range of male viewers between the ages of 18 to 55. The JetLev team sent Devin an email describing the effects of the video on their business. Devin's video had generated many more serious customer inquiries than even a four-minute piece that aired on several FOX television stations around the country. When compared to the quick, one-time exposure JetLev received from FOX, Devin's video kept generating interest. By August, the video had been viewed by 2 million people. By November, 3 million. By July 2012, 5.4 million viewers had watched Devin's Water Jet Pack video and were talking about it. That one video has 9,100 comments and counting. Who's watching that FOX news story today?

The partnership between Devin and JetLev is a duet—a simple brandscape. Devin got access to a $100,000 piece of equipment few people had ever seen, and JetLev got an awesome video that drives demand.

Devin's channel is successful for one major reason: he's got a hook and his audience loves it. His extreme music videos have generated 300 weekly subscribers and his videos have been viewed more than 56 million times. He's amassed a powerful audience in one year. If Devin sticks to his hook, exploits his format, and continues his success, he may surpass Red Bull's YouTube subscriber base by the end of 2012—all because he follows a formula for success.

Twist Until Your Hook Works

No matter what industry you're in, and no matter who your audience is, a hook makes your content worth subscribing to. It makes your content extremely hard to copy.

You have to force yourself to look for a hook. They don't come easy. It's a lot easier to decide you're going to do a documentary-style profile of an extreme athlete, than it is to say "we're going to push the boundaries of extreme sports each week with a new music video." But Devin's done it, and he's a "one-man band."

In the long run, building a format and creating a hook for your content actually makes content creation easier. It helps you and your brand partners focus on what you're doing and why you're working together.

If you're feeling stuck, just turn on the television to see how one format with a new hook can spawn a new show. *American Idol* is a reality television series that uses the audience to choose the next pop singing star. Take that format, give it another hook and you end up with NBC's *The Voice*. Twist it a little further and add karaoke to the mix and you get *Karaoke Battle USA*. Twist the show again for ballroom dancing, add some B-list celebrities, and you get *Dancing with the Stars*.

If you're creating content just for the sake of it, you're not building a content brand, you're acting like a news organization. This isn't sustainable or scalable, and it's extremely difficult to brandscape. (Hell, even news organizations are struggling with this.) However, a unique twist on the way your content is created can elevate your content from a commodity to an asset.

WHAT IF...

Devin Graham's extreme music videos are so well produced that he's created a loyal following of video production "gear heads." "Gear head" is an affectionate term for a videographer who wants to know how to better use his or her own equipment by understanding what "gear" and production techniques other videographers use.

After a few of his high-energy videos appeared on YouTube, Devin realized there was a whole subculture of extreme videographer gear heads interested in his production methods. They wanted to know what camera he was using and how he captured his extremely smooth motion shots.

That's when Devin started a second YouTube channel for "Behind the Scenes" videos. On Devin's second channel, he releases a corresponding video about how he made the music video you just watched. He gives you tips and tricks that go well beyond the gear he uses. He's personable and accessible. He's shedding light on the talent behind the content brand he's built.

Now, what if you manufacture video gear? What if you built a brandscape with Devin? Don't you think you could increase demand for the products you sell by showcasing what it can do as part of the final product?

On a recent shoot, Devin received a piece of production gear called a GoScope. The GoScope allows Devin to shoot from a unique perspective by attaching a camera to the end of a telescoping arm. He used the gear on a recent high-energy video and even let his viewers know how he got the unique shot in the video's description. Overnight, GoScope saw the power of Devin's video production skills and the "gear head" audience he's garnered. Sales of the GoScope tripled in one day.

(By the way, six months after Devin used the GoScope in his video, GoScope's website isn't even using the video to promote their product or Devin's videos on YouTube. If they were a good brandscaping partner, they'd be promoting Devin's work to their audience.)

Right now, Devin does all his YouTube channel videos for free. As long as someone can help him cover expenses, Devin will go anywhere and shoot anything, as long as it fits his content format and his unique hook. Devin treats his YouTube channel as a digital resume to help him get work as a photography director for commercial work.

He's just recently shot a commercial for Mountain Dew. So, his YouTube channel works.

But what if all of the manufacturers for the products Devin authentically endorses pooled their resources to turn his YouTube channel into a profit center of its own? Devin's spending a huge amount of time and energy creating these videos, and to great effect. It's driving demand for high-end cameras, accessories, lenses, and even clothes. Why couldn't the brands spend more time and energy putting their resources behind Devin (and people like him), instead of advertising in magazines and paying for Google AdWords?

Ask Yourself...

Who can help us brainstorm ideas to devise a good hook?

You've already started to identify talent that authentically believes in your brand. You've got a list of people who serve the same audience as you. You even know who owns your audience already. The fact is, you've got a team of resources waiting to share their ideas with anyone interested in seeing a rising tide. Use them.

Jet Lev didn't have the idea to create an awesome extreme music video—Devin Graham did. In every industry and for every brand, there are talented people willing to put their heads together to get creative, to make a mark and get results. All you have to do is be willing to listen, share your resources, and work together to find a hook, build a format, and brand your content.

In a world where brands like Quirky and Kickstarter (a crowd-funding website for creative projects) have built entirely new businesses based on the collaborative efforts of complete strangers, you don't have to do this alone—you can brandscape your way to a great hook.

Chapter 21
Make an Appointment with Your Audience

Carving Out Time

Once you've committed to building a content brand and have designed a format and a hook, you're ready to take the next step—you're ready to make an appointment with your audience.

Instead of contributing to information overload, your content must find its way into the content consumption habits of your target audience. You need to carve out some time in their minds so that they add your content to the list of things they want to consume on a regular basis.

Appointment Consumption

Appointment consumption is the notion that your audience expects the content they've grown to love on a predictable schedule. It could be a weekly sales tip, or a software tutorial delivered monthly. It could be a weekly live chat, a Tweet Up, or a photo of the day.

No medium pioneered the idea of appointment consumption better than television. And no one mastered the art better than a young television executive named Brandon Tartikoff.

Lessons from Must-See TV

In the early 80s, NBC was the lowest-rated broadcast television network until they hired Brandon Tartikoff, the youngest person to ever head their entertainment division. At age 31, Brandon decided that instead of trying to win every single night in the television ratings game, he'd just try to win one night. His goal was to get households around the country to tune-in on Thursday nights.

Brandon's efforts produced three of the most successful sitcoms in television history: *The Cosby Show, Family Ties,* and *Cheers.* These shows alone propelled NBC to the number one-rated television network by the end of the decade, and gave birth to the NBC slogan, "Must-See TV."

Brandon's strategy was based on "appointment television," a tried-and-true concept of television programming based on the idea that people will set aside a specific time and day to watch a program they've built a relationship with. While DVRs have allowed consumers to time-shift their content, and Internet video-viewing websites like Hulu, Netflix, and Amazon are making appointment television irrelevant, marketers can leverage the concept of appointment consumption to build their own successful social media platforms. In fact, everyone I've profiled so far in this book has done just that.

Remember *The Joe Show*—the example from the Advertising Specialty Institute (ASI) we talked about earlier? ASI has produced a highly formatted show that the audience expects every week. The only difference between their strategy and Brandon's is that the consumer has no idea what day *The Joe Show* will be released, but in an opt-in world, it doesn't matter.

Joe's episodes are delivered to the inboxes of his 800 subscribers every week. They don't know (or care) what day it is, but they've come to expect it. They've come to want it. They know that one day a week they'll get Joe's enthusiastic sales ideas via email, YouTube, the ASI newsletter, or a tweet. And they'll see it on their YouTube homepage when they're looking for something to watch.

Bob Knows Email

You can't build a relationship with an audience unless you deliver content on a regular schedule. This means you need to set the audience's expectation that they'll receive your content reliably. You've got to commit to your audience just like they are committing to you when they subscribe to your tweet stream, your YouTube channel, your blog, or your Facebook feed.

Take, for example, the longest-running email newsletter in the world: *Heard on the Web*, by Bob Sacks.

Every day, more than 16,000 executive and mid-level managers in the publishing industry receive three articles Bob knows will be relevant to his audience. Bob's opt-out rate is almost zero and his subscriber base is still growing. Bob's content has built a relationship with his audience since 1994—one that generates a large amount of revenue for Bob because there are plenty of people who want access to those 16,000 executives.

Every morning, when I open my email, there are three emails from Bob. I open and read every single one of them, every day. It's become a habit and I'm not alone. This kind of "habitual content consumption" creates a valuable relationship with the audience. *This* is appointment consumption.

You don't have to send content daily, like Bob does. You can send it weekly, monthly, semi-monthly, or even quarterly. But whatever frequency you choose, you must set—and then meet—the audience's expectations. If you find that your opt-out rate is too high, it doesn't mean you're sending out content too frequently. It means your content sucks or you're sending it to the wrong audience. Stop blaming your audience and start thinking like Bob.

Digital Stacking

There's another lesson we can learn from Brandon Tartikoff—one we can easily apply to the digital world. It's called stacking.

Stacking is the idea that if you put a few shows with similar themes together in one block of time you'll be able to maintain viewers for a longer period of time. Brandon knew that if he could get enough people to set aside 8 p.m. on Thursday nights to watch *The Cosby Show*, he could leverage the show's appeal to keep his viewers watching the same network for the next show. So he introduced *Family Ties*, which was followed up by *Cheers*. They were all versions of an ensemble, family-friendly cast getting a bit more "adult" as the evening progressed. Each show had a similar sitcom format, but each had a different hook.

Brandon's focus on creating a successful anchor in *The Cosby Show* for Thursday nights set in motion a two-decade-long string of television successes including a *Cheers* spin-off (*Frasier*), *Seinfeld*, and *Friends*. Brandon stacked more and more programming that leveraged the same audience for new content on a traditional media channel. The same concept can be applied to new media channel success, only this time around, we call it *digital* stacking.

The Joe Show has leveraged the success of Joe's original videos to create an entire spectrum of programming geared toward the same audience of specialty product professionals by highlighting even more focused niches within ASI's interests.

For example, did you know there's an entire promotional products category called "wearables"? I didn't either, but there is. ASI has created a new show featuring wearables editor C.J. Mittica reviewing the latest trends in logo-friendly wearables—things like hats, tank tops, and hunting gear. ASI has also launched an industry news program, and another series designed to deliver top sales tips from its industry's rock stars. These stacked shows are in their infancy today, but they all leverage the same principles of *The Joe Show's* success.

Ray William Johnson has also leveraged his digital success by stacking a whole new set of programs on top of his extremely successful =3 program. *Your Favorite Martian* (*YFM*) is a monthly animated video series that leverages original music by Ray and his gang to create really intriguing music videos that borrow from overused pop culture references (these videos are definitely not family friendly). During its first year, *YFM* generated 340 million views and today has nearly 2 million monthly subscribers.

Ray's also parlayed his =3 success into a web-based "serial reality show" titled *Breaking NYC,* which chronicles his everyday life. An additional 1 million fans have subscribed to it. The show follows Ray's many escapades and provides a behind-the-scenes look at =3 and *YFM*.

In total, leveraging the simple ideas of appointment consumption and digital stacking, Ray William Johnson has amassed an audience of 8 million regularly engaged people. Devin Graham has used his gear-head audience to stack a successful behind-the-scenes channel on top of his already successful extreme music videos.

Organizations like ASI and people like Ray and Devin are leveraging traditional television concepts to build media empires that drive demand for their content, expertise, and eventually, their products. That's right, even Ray William Johnson sells stuff like t-shirts, mugs, pins, posters, bracelets, and stickers. In the end, both *The Joe Show* and *=3* sell logo-laden promotional products.

The Joe Show, Devin Graham, and *=3* rely more on their social media platforms to build an audience than their websites. They're meeting the audience where they are by using appointment consumption—and keeping them there by employing digital stacking. It turns out that new media isn't that different from old media after all.

WHAT IF...

Joe Haley and Devin Graham have focused on delivering regularly scheduled content to drive their audience development strategy. But, what if there's a specific opportunity in the consumer's purchase process to leverage the concept of appointment consumption?

Homebuilder Catskill Farms has just such an opportunity.

Charles Petersheim has built a successful business in the foothills of the Catskill Mountains. He doesn't build homes for just anyone; instead, he has been designing "new, old homes" specifically for young professionals from New York City.

Sullivan County, where Petersheim builds his homes, is a two-hour drive from Manhattan. It's far enough to feel like you're away from the city, but not so far that you can't escape for a weekend. That two-hour drive meanders through New Jersey, up the Delaware River into Pennsylvania, then back into the New York hill country before you arrive at Catskill Farms.

What if Peter created a two-hour long audio podcast designed to highlight all the wonderful history, scenic overlooks, food stops, and shops his prospects pass on their way to his homes? What if each prospect was invited to download the podcast the minute they made an appointment to see a house? What if Charles partnered with the counties' tourism offices to put together a riveting two-hour tour that increased enthusiasm and even anticipation for what's ahead?

Appointment consumption relies on your ability to define a moment in time where your consumer can build a deeper relationship with your brand. What if you define one moment you can own?

Ask Yourself...

What is the best time for our content to be consumed?

I'm willing to bet you've never downloaded and dissected the data from the U.S. Department of Labor's American Time Use Survey (ATUS). That's okay, you can check out the 2008 data visualization on *The New York Times* website (http://bit.ly/atus2008).

Every four years, the federal government asks thousands of Americans to recall every minute of a day. The resulting insight provides us with an amazing deep dive into the time we spend eating, working, watching television, socializing, commuting, or even preparing dinner.

Here's the kind of nugget you can glean from the ATUS data: men, aged 25 to 64, are 1.5 times more likely to be using their computer between 8 p.m. and 10 p.m. That means, if you target that audience, you should strongly consider suggesting they consume your content during that timeframe.

Help your audience make time for your content. If you have an email newsletter targeted at those guys, don't you think it makes more sense to send it while they're at their computer? (That's not what the email gurus tell you—they say the "best" time for email open rates is between 2 p.m. and 5 p.m.)

The key here is to get to know your own particular audience. Ask yourself, when's the best time for *my* audience to make time for *my* content?

Chapter 22
Grow Rich, Target the Niche

Quality over Quantity

Twenty years ago, most major brands defined their audience or target customer by simply announcing things like gender, age range, household income, occupation, and perhaps the geographic location for their advertising buy. For example, say you wanted to reach male IT managers between the ages of 28 and 52, making over $100,000 a year. Any good media buyer would plug in your request to his or her software and tell you that your best bet would be to advertise in *Information Week.*

Today, there are hundreds of thousands of websites, content creators, YouTubers, bloggers, screen-casters, podcasters, and eBook writers that attract small niches within the IT market. No one can understand the broad customer base the way we defined it 20 years ago. Nowadays, you must focus on very specific, highly valuable fragments of a broadly defined population.

The fact is, your customers and clients can find content that speaks specifically to them in today's web world. So if you're targeting too broad of an audience, you're not going to be relevant to anyone. The deeper you define your niche, the more relevant you'll be—albeit to a smaller audience. But you'll make a bigger impact.

You have to start considering the quality of the audience you reach instead of the quantity of people you reach. You have to consider the quality of the relationships you're building with your customers, clients, and prospects, instead of the quantity of impressions you've garnered.

Niche targeting is unbelievably successful if you care about quality over quantity. Just ask the Chicken Whisperer and the folks at Tractor Supply.

The Chicken Whisperer

Andy Schneider is the Chicken Whisperer. That doesn't mean he can communicate with chickens—it's the brand he's built for himself.

Andy dubs himself the "go-to guy across the country for anything chicken-related."

Andy's not a career chicken farmer; in fact, he lives in a suburban Atlanta home where he raises a dozen-or-so chickens. He's a former paramedic and corporate consultant, and since 2007, he's been broadcasting his own radio show about raising backyard poultry.

For the uninitiated, the backyard poultry movement started gaining momentum at the turn of this century. In urban areas around the nation, regular city-dwellers and suburban homeowners raise their own poultry, primarily as pets. (The fact that the chickens lay eggs is a nice side benefit.)

As Andy's passion for his own backyard brood grew, he started a radio show on an Atlanta AM radio station broadcasting live every Saturday. Other Atlanta-area backyard poultry enthusiasts would call in and ask Andy or his expert guests questions about anything chicken-related.

Andy also started a local-area Meetup group (using Meetup.com) and held monthly meetings for his fans, friends, fellow poultry enthusiasts, and local chicken experts. Andy was successfully developing a nice following, but even with a few thousand weekly listeners, his efforts weren't going to pay the bills. (His audience wasn't big enough to attract real sponsor dollars.)

That's when Andy realized that if he could scale his radio show he could attract an audience from around the country. If there were 2,000 weekly listeners in Atlanta, could he get the same number in 10 other cities? Surely, 20,000 poultry enthusiasts would be valuable to someone.

Each night for a week, Andy scoured the Internet looking for an easy way to broadcast around the globe and that's when he found BlogTalkRadio.com (which today is the largest and fastest growing online talk radio network). After a few experiments broadcasting on the Internet to his wife listening in the other room, Andy was ready to take his two-hour radio show global.

Every weekday (yes, five days a week), Andy chats about keeping backyard poultry. Whether you're raising "show" poultry, trying to live a self-sufficient lifestyle, or just keeping a few chickens as pets, Andy and his guests answer your questions and share stories from the backyard poultry movement.

Today, 636 episodes after he started, Andy's audience tops out at well over 20,000 backyard poultry enthusiasts from around the world. "We have truck drivers and school teachers, urban chicken enthusiasts and vegans, that all listen to our show," Andy says. There are even "feed and seed" stores around the country that stream the radio show live over PA systems every day from noon to 2 p.m.

Andy says that 70 percent of the listeners are women between the ages of 35 and 55 who have an average of a dozen (or fewer) chickens at home. "Most of our listeners see their chickens as pets. They could never imagine eating precious 'Petunia.' These are suburban homeowners who love their chickens just like their neighbors love their dogs," he adds.

Andy's Meetup groups have grown, too. Today, you can join a "Backyard Poultry Meetup Group" in Austin (1,200 members) or Boston (266 members) where online enthusiasts can meet offline to trade poultry secrets. Andy's online broadcasting success has translated into a real-world fan base and even a book. *The Chicken Whisperer's Guide to Keeping Chickens* is his go-to manual for getting started in the backyard poultry world.

The Chicken Whisperer's radio show has a long list of sponsors that have tapped into the community Andy's created. His traditional advertisers range from chicken feed manufacturers to online retailers, like MyPetChicken.com.

Andy's been able to attract radio show sponsors by highlighting the quality of his niche audience. Thanks to the web, he's been able to attract a large-enough audience to be valuable to a very specific set of brands. Each of his audience members is obviously interested in one thing: chickens. Which means the advertisers are always relevant to the audience he serves. Unlike your morning drive-time radio show, he's not trying to be everything to everyone.

Andy Schneider has tapped into a passionate niche of consumers and he's built a relationship with them through his daily radio show. But one specific retailer has turned the Chicken Whisperer's audience into an unbelievably powerful marketing and sales partnership.

Facilitating the Meet & Greet

The Chicken Whisperer has a ton of existing radio show sponsors but the power of his platform can really be seen when it's tied to driving customers into a retail store where you can really measure Andy's impact.

Tractor Supply is the largest retail "farm and ranch" store chain in the United States. With more than 1,000 retail stores in 44 states, it's a $4 billion business.[29] Most of their stores are located in rural areas or the outlying suburbs of major American cities. At any one of their stores, you can find everything from welding supplies and riding lawn mowers, to fashion-forward men's and women's work wear. What's interesting about Tractor Supply is that they target the "hobby farmer." They say that less than 10 percent of their clients describe themselves as full-time farmers or ranchers. They are "suburban homeowners" or "self-reliants." That sounds exactly like the Chicken Whisperer's audience.

Almost every week, Andy and his family hit the road with his radio show. Armed with a microphone, headphones, and a laptop, Andy can broadcast from almost anywhere (that's the power of BlogTalkRadio). A few years ago, he even broadcast from his car on the way to Nashville. When Andy comes to town, it's a big deal in the backyard poultry community. Listeners and fans from all over come to see Andy live and in-person.

For a meager appearance fee, Andy brings his radio show to stores including Tractor Supply. He spends the day there, signing books, broadcasting his show, even hosting a "getting started" workshop for backyard poultry newbies. It's an event. At any given appearance, Andy draws 40 to 300 new customers, many of whom have never visited a Tractor Supply in their life.

Next thing you know they're purchasing a dozen baby chicks, chicken coops, chicken feed, incubators, and poultry supplies galore. Andy easily sells 100 new chicks at an appearance, and sometimes they sell out fast. The typical chicken owner spends $144 on feed alone each year. That means if Andy brings in 300 new customers, he just drove more than $40,000 in annual revenue for each Tractor Supply he visits in one day (not to mention all the other stuff poultry enthusiasts purchase over the course of their chick's lifetime). By the way, chickens can easily live eight to 10 years, which means that over the life of the chickens, Andy sells $400,000 worth of chicken feed at each store he visits.

Tractor Supply has been so successful working with Andy, that it even has a special section on its website featuring introductory backyard poultry videos and advice. Mannapro, a feed sponsor, has a special "Ask the Chicken Whisperer" section on its website, too, offering direct access to Andy's insight and knowledge.

It's a perfect example of a brandscape. Andy gets to connect with his audience. Tractor Supply drives new revenue and forms relationships with customers who had never considered visiting their store. Mannapro gets exposed to new poultry enthusiasts the minute they start considering raising chickens. Together, they grow Andy's exposure on their websites. Website visitors get access to personalized, branded content from a trusted source, while Tractor Supply gets great content that drives interest from a passionate consumer base devoted to backyard poultry.

Tractor Supply understands the value of Andy's high-quality niche audience and they've tapped into it in a completely authentic way. The result has been a successful partnership that benefits both parties.

While Andy's in any given town, he's usually trailed by the local news media. He's something of a media darling, having appeared on CNN and in *USA Today*, *TIME*, and *The Economist*. The additional exposure certainly doesn't hurt.

See for yourself. Sign up for the Chicken Whisperer's newsletter (http://bit.ly/chickenwhisperer) and go meet him when he's in your neighborhood.

You'll see—it's marketing symbiosis at its best.

Helping Them Help You

Tractor Supply has taken advantage of the opportunity to help Andy Schneider grow his audience because it increases demand for the products they sell at their retail outlets. Even browsing their website's "Know-How Central" section, it's easy to see how attaching a personal brand like the Chicken Whisperer to their Poultry Care content brings their brand, and their content, to life.

Instead of trying to inauthentically create poultry-oriented content for their audience, Tractor Supply partnered with the most credible brand in the marketplace—one with a rabid audience to boot. If Tractor Supply took the same approach with everything from "Cattle Care" to "Rabbit Care," they'd have a richer, more personable and powerful digital experience that marries directly to an offline marketing program designed to drive people into their stores.

You, too, need to start breaking down your audience to understand where their passions lie. Like Tractor Supply, you cannot be everything to everyone. Start with one niche at a time, find a Chicken Whisperer in your world, and design ways to authentically integrate your audiences all the way to the point of purchase. The results will be phenomenal.

When you design a strategy like this, you need to think long term. Tractor Supply doesn't look at their relationship with Andy Schneider as a "campaign." Andy's invited to stop by a Tractor Supply at any time.

"Sometimes, I find myself on the road without a place to do the show and I just call up Tractor Supply. They get me in touch with the local store manager and next thing you know I'm bringing people to a store I hadn't planned on visiting," Andy says. That's a real relationship. Tractor Supply wants the backyard poultry people to build a relationship through Andy with their brand today, tomorrow, and next year.

Andy's relationships with his sponsors have built him a business born out of his passion for backyard poultry. He makes more money than he ever did as a paramedic (and most of his years as a corporate consultant).

I guarantee there is a sea of passionate customers and clients trying to turn their hobbies and passions into viable businesses that could increase demand for your products. What are you doing to help *them* help *you*?

WHAT IF...

What's next for the Chicken Whisperer? Andy's far from making his passion a long-term and vibrant business. He's embraced the radio show as a lifestyle choice. But he's full of energy and ideas. Once a month, he says, he's approached by a television network or producer about turning his life into a television show. The problem is, they're trying to make him into something he's not.

"If you're looking for a redneck, backwoods, chicken farmer who can tell your rooster's fortune, you've got the wrong guy," Andy says of the discussions he's had with television producers. But if you were Tractor Supply or even Ace Hardware or Mannapro, wouldn't you like to see "Bob Villa for the Backyard Poultry World"? That's how Andy sees his program. It's full of adventure, traveling the country, and meeting backyard enthusiasts fighting City Hall to ensure that backyard chicken farmers have their rights.

Andy's proven that you don't need a big media conglomerate to make a daily radio show a success. So why would he need a broadcast network to make his television show a viable option?

In the short term, Andy's looking for a better way to travel with his radio show. What if you were a recreational vehicle (RV) manufacturer? What if you helped Andy hit the road and stop at every single Tractor Supply store in the nation? What if Andy's weekly road trip was part of your brandscape strategy?

What if you learned more about your niche content creators and started to uncover *their* needs?

Ask Yourself...

Which niche should we go after first?

If you're going to start targeting niche markets—and I'm talking "backyard poultry" niche—you'll need to get a handle on the quality of the audience the niche has garnered. How passionate are they?

Obviously, Andy's poultry-lovin' audience is passionate and committed, but if you sell services to small businesses, where can you find that kind of passionate niche? Instead of just saying you target small business owners, keep asking yourself "what kind." Are you targeting the owners of small banks? Franchise owners? These are examples of niches with passionate professionals at the helm. Are you going to be more successful targeting the audience that reads *Community Banking*—or *Franchise Times*? Only you can answer that question. Either way, I guarantee you'll be more successful than if you just target "all small business owners."

Chapter 23
Create a Movement, Tap a Trend

Solidifying a Passion Point

Andy Schneider had the benefit of hooking his coat tails on the rise of the backyard poultry movement. Maybe, just maybe, Andy Schneider, *is* the backyard poultry movement. If you asked the media, they certainly see him that way. He's the mouthpiece for a generation of suburban families that want to know where their food is coming from. As Andy often says, his "eggs travel 30 feet from farm to table, instead of 1,500 miles." He knows exactly what went into the hens so he knows exactly what he gets out.

But what about your industry? Have you considered what kind of niche movement you can identify, power, or scale?

Most brands aren't taking the time to understand and identify opportunities to tap into the passions of your audience and turn those passions into a movement. Most brands try to turn trends into campaigns. They try to capitalize on the passion of an existing audience and idea by branding it as their own. This doesn't work in a social media world. It's inauthentic. It's a turn off.

The better approach is to offer your resources, support, and advice when you identify a trend, movement, or a passion point. As a result, you'll see organic growth of your customer base and the category as a whole. You can do the same thing with multiple niches. Doesn't that sound more appealing than investing in a campaign that drains resources, dilutes authenticity, and reeks of manufactured-brand interaction?

There are passionate movements underneath every single market, industry, product, and brand. You just have to look hard to find them. Breville, an Australian-based, kitchen appliance manufacturer, has an amazing story to tell. A story based entirely on the passion of one brand advocate and his belief that he could help people live healthier lives.

Fat, Sick & Nearly Dead

Breville sells kitchen countertop appliances. They sell espresso machines, panini presses, slow cookers, and toaster ovens among other things. For years they've also sold juicers. For a company that's been around for more than 70 years, they're relatively new to the U.S. market.

Jack LaLanne popularized the idea of juicing fruits and vegetables using a series of infomercials in the 1980s. Since then, Breville and other brands have sold millions of juicers around the world.

Rob Sheard, Breville's brand director, recognized that most Breville juicers were purchased around New Years. "It's like a gym membership. People make a resolution to live a more healthy lifestyle. They join a gym or buy a juicer and commit for a couple of months." The juicer business has been growing slowly over the last few years, and as Rob says, today, it's a $70 million to $80 million appliance category nationwide.

Breville's marketing team gets hundreds of unsolicited requests for kitchen appliances each and every week. "We have to say no to most of them, but in 2010, we got a call from an Australian documentary filmmaker who wanted a Breville juicer. His project sounded interesting so we sent him one," Rob says.

That Australian filmmaker was Joe Cross. At 310 pounds, Joe needed to change his life. He was 100 pounds overweight, suffered from a debilitating chronic disease, and his doctors had loaded him up on medication. Joe decided he would trade in his junk food diet for a juicer and vowed to drink only fresh juice for 60 days straight. He flew to the United States, bought a car, mounted his juicer (and a generator) in the back, and headed off on a cross-country journey to heal his lifestyle.

At a truck stop in Arizona, Joe met a truck driver named Phil Staples. Phil suffered from the same disease as Joe. He was morbidly obese (at 429 pounds) and he wasn't happy with his lifestyle, either. Together, Joe and Phil built a new outlook on life. They built a strong bond, and the documentary covers every twist and turn. The result is a feature-length documentary called *Fat, Sick & Nearly Dead.*

Fat, Sick & Nearly Dead is uplifting, inspiring, fun, and heartwarming. It's an emotional story about how you have to change your lifestyle if you're going to lose weight, build your self-esteem, and live a healthier life. It's about real people, making real changes that affect not only their lives, but the lives they touch.

During the production of the film, one of Breville's marketing staff had kept in touch with Joe, primarily on Facebook. Rob Sheard was excited about the film, but wondered how it would get distribution. Rob's reservations weren't unfounded. *Fat, Sick & Nearly Dead* would have to be picked up by a national film distributor and shown in at least 230 movie theaters to mimic the success of other documentary films like *Super Size Me*. This would be no easy task.

But Joe and his team live in a world where relying on traditional media distribution is no longer a requirement. Instead of hoping to appear in movie theaters, Joe and his producers opted to distribute the movie online, streaming it on Hulu, Amazon, and Netflix.

When the film was released on Netflix, during the first week of July 2011, the impact was immediate. "Our website went crazy," Rob says. "Within three weeks, our entire juicer stock was sold out nationwide and the demand kept growing. Nine months later, we were still struggling to keep up."

As Rob points out, the more popular a film is on a platform like Netflix, the more often it's referenced, which makes it more popular. Nine months after the movie was released, it was still being reviewed almost daily on Netflix. At the time of this writing, more than 1,700 people had *Fat, Sick & Nearly Dead* in their "watch instantly" cue on Netflix alone.[30]

Netflix's 24 million subscribers, watching a 97-minute documentary, increased demand for Breville's line of juicers more than any ad campaign the company had ever run, and it's lasted longer, too.

"Besides partnering with Joe Cross' company, Join The Reboot, to share in the revenue they drive, we've supported Joe's grassroots efforts to get the film out there," Rob says.

Essentially, for a free juicer and some goodwill, Breville has never seen such high demand for juicers. That's a pretty good return on investment, if you ask me.

Tapping Into a Trend

While it's Breville juicers that are seen in the film *Fat, Sick & Nearly Dead*, the movie has had a mammoth impact on the juicing market at large. The film itself increased demand for the lifestyle the film portrays. Buying a juicer is only one piece of the puzzle. If you're going to juice, you need to buy fruits and vegetables. That's why the high-end, grocery chain, Whole Foods, has held screenings of the film at their stores.

As Rob points out, this trend was waiting for a personality to bring it to market: "Odwala's been selling all-natural fresh-fruit drinks in more and more stores. Starbucks recently announced the launch of a series of fresh juice bars. Burger King is offering fresh fruit smoothies. Walmart is popularizing the idea of organic fruits and vegetables. Joe Cross brought all of these trends together in a way that anyone could identify with—he showcased the impact these choices have on our lives. He put a face to the trend."

What's next for the Breville team? Sure they could increase their advertising for juicers, or spend money on branding to take credit for the movement (like a traditional marketer might). But instead, they're planning to put more marketing muscle into *Fat, Sick & Nearly Dead*. They're going to help Joe get the word out by pooling their resources to purchase some advertising for the movie.

The more people who see the film, the more juicers they'll sell. Now, instead of seeing a spike only around New Year's resolution time, Breville can enjoy an ever-increasing demand for juicers that *Fat, Sick & Nearly Dead* has created.

Remember the impact that *Finding Nemo* had on the demand for clownfish? *Fat, Sick & Nearly Dead* takes advantage of the very same phenomenon and leverages it to change lives and sell products.

Put Their Passion First

Let's be honest—Breville got lucky. Joe Cross turned out to be a talented filmmaker with the resources available to make his movie a success. All Breville had to do was give him a free juicer and some moral support. But if you look hard enough, you too can find these types of brandscaping opportunities.

No trend is too small to move your market. Get to know the people who buy your products. What underlying reasons do they have for embracing your value proposition? What can you do to support personalities who have a knack for telling your story?

One piece of content can increase demand for a product or product category—it can happen any time, in any market. Look at the cupcake craze Carrie Bradshaw created after her visit to the Magnolia Bakery on *Sex and the City*—it's still going strong six years later. Rap musicians have long influenced their fans' purchasing habits, helping sell Courvoisier, champagne, other people's music, Nike shoes, clothing, and even dental wear. Oprah Winfrey has turned struggling companies into powerhouse brands.

The only difference between these examples and today's reality is that you don't need *Sex and the City*, a rap star, or Oprah to peddle your brand. There are content creators on the other side of every web link looking for a way to tell your story.

Don't tell me you can't find these people. If you can't find these people, you're targeting too big of a market or too large of an audience. Joe Cross didn't make a kitchen appliance movie. He didn't make a movie for all kinds of juicing enthusiasts. Actually, Joe Cross didn't make a movie about juicing at all. Joe Cross made a movie about changing your life. It just so happens that he changed his life by juicing.

Stop putting your product first and start putting the passions and motivations of your audience first. You'll connect with your market and reap the rewards of helping people understand how your products and services can impact their lives.

Even Rob Sheard accepts the possibility that there's a story for every product category Breville sells. "I can't imagine a documentary about how toaster ovens can change your life, but you never know," he says.

As a brandscaper, think of these trend-driven opportunities as a hedge fund. Invest in a few different niches with a few different people. Help them tell their stories or create their content. The more diversified your investments, the higher the likelihood you'll see a success story like Breville's.

WHAT IF...

What if Breville embraced the idea that they could capitalize on a movement or a trend that supported every one of their product lines? What if they decided they were going to capitalize on the cupcake trend to sell mixers? What if they decided to create a panini movement to sell more sandwich presses?

Kathy Strahs *is* Panini Happy. She's a prolific and award-winning blogger who creates, photographs, and posts amazingly creative and scrumptious panini recipes every week.

It all started a few years ago when Kathy received a Breville panini grill as a gift from her sister and, while she was grateful, she couldn't help but think, "Uh oh...you know I'm gonna use this once and then add it to the appliance wasteland that is my pantry. That's what I did with the ice cream maker, the crepe machine, the pizzelle machine—and those are the ones I can at least remember."

That's when she vowed to break the cycle. She decided to start a panini blog. "Each experiment is like a little project that I get to conceptualize, execute—and eat! It may be the job I've been looking for all my life," she says.

Her blog's a great success, attracting tens of thousands of readers every month.[31] She's been featured in *The New York Times*, *Saveur Magazine*, even a local parenting magazine in San Diego, her hometown.

Kathy helps consumers maintain their enthusiasm and inspiration for a countertop appliance that might have otherwise been relegated to the back of the pantry. Kathy increases interest in paninis.

One of the most interesting concepts Kathy has introduced to her fans is the Panini Party. It's a simple concept really. Put out a panini press and a whole host of delectable ingredients, perhaps a few inspirational recipe ideas, and let your guests go to work.

"I've hosted more than a dozen [panini parties], usually combined with a movie," says one of Kathy's Facebook fans. "I generally have a set recipe for everyone, and it's fun to experiment with themes and ingredients."

What if Breville powered panini parties around the world? What if they helped Kathy expand her reach and inspired their hundreds of thousands of customers to break out the panini press for their next event?

What if Breville helped Kathy publish a panini party book (she has a panini recipe book coming out in 2013)? What if Breville and Kathy worked with Williams-Sonoma (who sells Breville products) to put together a panini party package?

What if you tapped a trend and helped support a movement that increases demand for your products?

Ask Yourself...

Where can we start to uncover the movements and trends that might move our market?

Sometimes, all a trend needs to gain momentum is a brand's willingness to help see it succeed. Uncovering these consumer-driven movements has never been easier, and tracking them is free.

Start watching for relevant trends while you consume content from the brands, influencers, and consumers that you're already following. Start making a list of these trends and the instances where you observe them. Include any ideas that come to you during this process.

Next, experiment with Google Insights For Search (http://bit.ly/analyzegoogleinsights). Google Insights allows you to track the evolution of a trend by studying consumer search data.

For example, if I sell garden supplies, flowers, seeds, and shrubs, I might have noticed that some of my influential content creators have been writing about "living walls," or wall gardens. Using Google Insights, I can see that since 2009, searches for "living walls" has doubled, and the trend is forecast to continue.

This means that anything I can do to help more people embrace the idea of building a living wall will sell more garden supplies.

Don't take a mere mention of a new idea from an influential partner for granted—it just may be the next big thing.

Chapter 24
Exploit Content Holes

The 200 Channel Universe

In a world where consumers have access to more and more information, you have to focus on a smaller, higher-quality, audience. In other words, you have to identify—and exploit—the content holes in your market. Lauren Luke did it when she created her celebrity-inspired video tutorials (none of the major makeup brands were helping teenage girls create looks inspired by their idols). The Advertising Specialty Institute (ASI) did it when they created the *The Joe Show* (no one else in their market was creating videos to help people sell more promotional products).

But how do you find content holes when there are so many outlets out there? Sometimes you stumble upon them by mistake.

I Want My FishTV

Cable television in the mid-90s was expanding at a rapid pace. In the news and information channel line-up alone, that decade saw the debut of MSNBC, Fox News, CNNSI (Sports Illustrated), and CNN Headline News. The average television consumer started to wonder who would consume all this information.

Meanwhile, in Columbia, South Carolina, the team at the local Cablevision provider began marketing the latest addition its cable line-up, the Sci Fi Network. The local marketing team had spent a considerable amount of money advertising the new network to existing subscribers who were eagerly awaiting the channel's premiere.

Unfortunately, only days before the channel was to go live, the Cablevision team learned that they hadn't secured the necessary approvals from the FCC to take the channel live. They'd have to delay the premiere until everything had been checked and re-checked.

With a channel all ready to go and a customer base eager to tune in, the team needed something to put on the empty channel. With only hours to spare, they rolled a fish tank into the studio and turned the camera on. Anyone tuning in to what was supposed to be reruns of *Star Trek*, would instead be treated to a 24-hour live-stream of the company's fish tank, with a scrolling message explaining the situation.

The company had prepared for the backlash of angry customers desperate to see their Sci Fi favorites, but the phones and fax machines were silent. What had gone wrong? Was their marketing a failure?

Months later, after all the appropriate approvals were received, Columbia Cablevision flipped the switch, turning off their streaming fish tank and turning on the Sci Fi Network. There was little fanfare and no marketing of the new network. They didn't expect much.

When management came into the office the next day, their answering machine was full and the fax machine was overflowing with pleas from cable subscribers demanding their "Fish TV" be turned back on. With no market research and no prescribed consumer demand, Columbia Cablevision had found an audience for a channel with a live-streaming fish tank and nothing more. They'd invented FishTV.

The backlash was so fervent that the Cablevision team struck a deal with the Bravo network, which, at the time, had no original daytime programming. During the day, they could stream FishTV, and at night they could switch back to Bravo's programming. The resourceful team even found a local aquarium purveyor to sponsor and maintain the fish tank. Completely by accident, they'd turned a marketing disaster into a revenue stream with an audience that at least one local business owner found valuable.

The Crowded Market Paradox

Paradoxically, the more information sources available to the consumer, the more niche-focused content creators must become and the more successful they'll be. Even in a world with 44 billion indexed web pages in Google's database, content opportunities like FishTV exist. You, as a marketer, have to find and exploit these content holes in your marketplace.

While the publishing industry wallows in a proliferation of people proclaiming the death of print, many publishers are seeing continued success. Take, for example, niche publisher *FIDO Friendly* magazine (check them out at http://www.fidofriendly.com).

There are plenty of general-interest travel magazines and even a few giant digital platforms that own the travel space. There are also tons of general-interest pet magazines. However, no one—literally no one— targeted the 29 million Americans who travel each year with their pets. That's where *FIDO Friendly* came in.

Whether you travel with a Shih Tzu or a Rottweiler, *FIDO Friendly* has advice, insight, reviews, tips, trends, and even product recommendations to make your pet traveling adventures easier and more rewarding. A recent issue included a feature cover story about actress Betty White, who brings her pets everywhere she goes. Who knew?

FIDO Friendly does its own *Consumer Reports*-style car reviews with a focus on comfort, space, and amenities for your road-tripping pet. The staff curates destination reviews and highlights hotels, restaurants, and service providers that will cater to your pet's every whim. The magazine has been so successful that it's launched two radio shows: Pet Life Radio and Animal Radio, which airs on XM Satellite and attracts 500,000 weekly listeners.

FIDO Friendly is the complete opposite of a general-interest travel rag. In fact, if I travel with my bird or my cat, *FIDO Friendly* isn't even for me. FIDO Friendly is an extremely successful, niche-focused publication, digital platform, and now radio network, that attracts a loyal, passionate fan base of valuable consumers.

General-interest magazines and newspapers are dying for one simple reason: in a world where loyal consumers follow and consume information about their passions, their professions, their companies, and their industries, pursuing a general-interest content strategy is a huge mistake. Advertising and marketing on these platforms no longer makes sense.

Embrace Fractal Marketing

To be successful identifying the content holes in your marketplace, you'll need to accept that the digital content world is infinitely divisible, a concept called *fractal marketing*.

In other words, your content can be targeted and contextualized to meet an infinitely divisible audience. Just like *FIDO Friendly* looked at the opportunities in the travel space as an opportunity to create content for a very specific kind of traveler (one who travels with their dog), you can split and splice your audience to ensure the content you deliver is relevant. The more your content "speaks to" your audience, the more they'll embrace your brand and the content creator who brings it to them.

The more you subdivide your audience, the more valuable it gets. Sure, *National Geographic Traveler* magazine may have a huge subscriber base, but if you're trying to position your hotel as pet-friendly, where are your dollars best spent? *National Geographic Traveler* or *FIDO Friendly*? Which audience will be more valuable? Where will your brand be more relevant, more often? Who's going to cut through the clutter?

Imagine for a moment a picture of a tree. The trunk of the tree forks into a series of branches. Now, in your mind, crop and rotate the picture of the tree so that one of the branches now looks like the trunk from the larger image. This "new" trunk now forks into a series of branches. Crop and rotate, again. And again. Any tree branch, when magnified and rotated, looks like the entire tree. This phenomenon of self-similar repeating patterns is called a "fractal."

The world wide web is no different. Pick any tree trunk of web content—like travel (see Figure 5). Immediately, you can branch the tree into business or leisure travel. Both of these branches have wildly different audiences.

Now, zoom-in on leisure travel. Crop and rotate so you treat it like a trunk. Divide leisure travel into two branches: "adventure leisure" and "relaxing leisure."

Again, these are both types of travel, but the audiences are completely different. If you divide and subdivide deep enough, you end up with

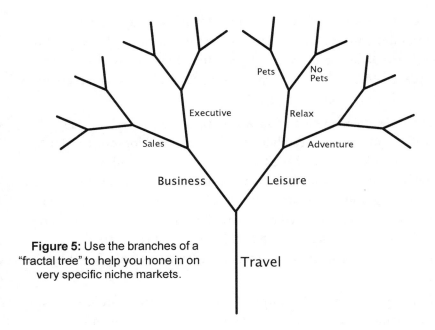

Pets

No Pets

Executive

Relax

Sales

Adventure

Business

Leisure

Figure 5: Use the branches of a "fractal tree" to help you hone in on very specific niche markets.

Travel

FRACTAL MARKETING

"relaxing-leisure travel with your dog." Where can you find that audience? *FIDO Friendly* magazine or FIDOFriendly.com. This is the power of fractal marketing.

When you start thinking in terms of fractal marketing, you'll find yourself in a universe of content creators already reaching an audience relevant to your brand. The trick is to find a node on the tree that's big enough to target, but small enough to be relevant to on a regular basis. Targeting the right node on a fractal web world makes you, your brand, and your content more relevant, more often.

I'm willing to bet that no matter what you sell, or what services you provide, there are at least 10 niche websites, all with valuable audiences, where you can acquire new customers and continually grow your business.

Assume you sell hats. Or maybe you realize that your audience loves hats. What does the digital hat universe look like? First of all there's *Hat Magazine* (TheHatMagazine.com). The magazine staff also runs a consumer forum called HatsUK.com. There's a group on Flickr that features more than 21,100 images of hats and currently boasts 3,400 members. Darla Sycamore, a self-proclaimed Hat Revivalist, runs a blog called Many Hatty Returns (For the Love of Hats) and even offers a free VIP newsletter subscription.

There are amazing niche sites within these niche sites, like Church Hats By Lola (you can read her stuff at ladieshats.blogspot.com). Or maybe you like tiny hats? Well then, you should be reading TinyHatsWeekly.com, where they feature images and notes about tiny hats ranging from miniature pirate hats to hats for cats. There's even a YouTube channel dedicated to videos of crocheted hats (imagine how great it would be to stumble upon this channel if you were the manufacturer of crochet supplies like needles and yarn!). I could go on and on.

Want a more practical example? Okay. I met a merchandise manager for Williams-Sonoma, a retailer that sells gourmet foods and professional-quality cookware. She was lamenting that sales of their tea merchandise were waning, even as more consumers are drinking tea. Williams-Sonoma sells tea kettles, fancy tea leaves, all sorts of tea cups and saucers, not-to-mention tea pots. I asked her if she'd ever heard of Steepster.com.

Steepster.com is an online community of tea lovers who keep digital journals of the teas they drink. Members can review teas and even recommend teas to others in the community. By early 2012, Steepster's community had written more than 100,000 tasting notes on more than 28,000 different teas! Had she ever heard of it? No.

Well, I think it's pretty obvious that if you want to sell more tea merchandise, you'd better spend some time on Steepster. If you want the tea community to embrace your brand, you'd better embrace the tea aficionados. If you want to encourage the tea community to visit Williams-Sonoma, you'd better add Steepster to your list of brandscaping opportunities.

Do you see how diving into the fractal web universe by better understanding the niches your audience is passionate about will help you pinpoint content holes to exploit? If you can't find a content hole, you either don't understand your customers, or you haven't dug deep enough into their content consumption habits.

Imagine if you could harness the power of one community (a node on your fractal tree) to grow sales even one percent. What would happen if you participated in 10 communities? Ten percent growth?

WHAT IF...

Joe Cross filled a content hole with his feature-length film *Fat, Sick & Nearly Dead*. Andy Schneider, the Chicken Whisperer, found an audience of backyard poultry enthusiasts. Kathy (Panini Happy) Strahs captured the attention of those interested in grilled sandwiches. All of these people found a niche market for their content and drove sales for the companies in their respective brandscapes. Content holes aren't easy to find. Often times it takes a lot of experimentation and patience to create content that sticks.

Looking for a short cut to identifying content holes? Look no further than your industry's trade magazines. What topics are not covered frequently enough? What topics drove a lot of demand in the past? What if you took the reigns and started delivering that content, with a talented persona attached, more frequently? And what if that content helped your audience grow their business?

Robert H. Ham Store Fixtures helps retailers display their wares. They sell everything from mannequins and racks to cases and shelves. In May 2012, they began providing "retail tips" at their website. Robert H. Ham has obviously found a content hole in the marketplace. Indeed a quick review of the trade magazines in their space reveals a lack of frequently published, practical ideas for retailers on how to improve their sales through the use of more effective displays.

However, there are a few problems with Robert H. Ham's content: there's no discernable, trusted talent attached to the "tips" (in fact, this section of the site isn't even called a blog); the stock images are inauthentic; and the quality of the content isn't any better than what you can find elsewhere.

What if Robert H. Ham partnered with a retail design expert to create really great content? In particular, I'm thinking of someone like Lynne Mesher, who wrote a fantastic article about retail design "on a dime" for the *NICHE* Magazine website in 2010.

Lynne's a retail designer and educator who's written a book titled, "*Basics Interior Design: Retail Design.*" What if Robert H. Ham gave away a free copy of her book with orders of a certain dollar value? What if they helped Lynne build a retail design blog (as far as I can tell, Lynne doesn't blog)? What if they really started working with Lynne, and other experts like her, to provide their customers with valuable information that would make their jobs easier?

What if *you* used your industry magazines and associations to help identify content holes? Could you drive more business?

Ask Yourself...

What have we seen, online or off, that might help us identify a content hole?

No matter what business you're in, I guarantee there are customers and clients using your ideas or products in ways you've never imagined. I'm also willing to bet they're sharing those ideas in a close-knit community on a fractal node you might never have explored. These people, and the communities in which they participate, can help you identify existing content holes. So where are they?

Trade magazines, seemingly off-topic websites, niche publications, online forums, and social media channels are the gateway to these people and their inspiration. Explore these channels and when you find offbeat ideas, post them on a corkboard (no idea is too small or too weird to ignore!). Look for patterns in the content you find. Group the ideas by audience type or by idea. There are no shortcuts to identifying a content hole, but it's like dating, you'll know it when you see it.

In 2006, a woman who goes by the online pseudonym "Jules," found herself searching for unique ways to decorate her house. On blog-after-blog and in forum-after-forum she found hundreds of online tutorials that transformed off-the-shelf IKEA items into original furniture, lighting, and design elements. Lucky for Jules, she lives only 15 minutes from an IKEA, so she could easily try out many of the ideas she was finding. Not long after, she started IKEAHackers.net.

Today, people from around the globe submit their IKEA hacks to Jules' website. It's become an online resource for an unbelievable array of projects that all start with a trip to IKEA. IKEA hacking has become a cultural meme for a generation of college graduates furnishing their first apartment. And guess what? IKEA hackers, as they're now called, purchase tons of IKEA products.

Jules found a content hole in the marketplace and she exploited it by bringing together an entire community to form a valuable node (people looking for creative ways to use IKEA products) on IKEA's fractal tree. What if IKEA had been looking for content holes and had found those early hackers before Jules did? What if IKEA started to feature hacks in their annual catalogs? Wouldn't they sell more furniture, fixtures, and encourage more innovation? Jules has no affiliation with IKEA. Why they're not supporting her endeavor right now, I can't explain.

Where are your "IKEA hackers"? Where are all the people who already embrace the types of products and services you sell, and what are they passionate about? They're out there and they have the potential to grow your audience, drive new revenue, and redefine your business. You just have to find them.

As you surf the web, do so with the intention of connecting the dots between the seemingly disparate content you collect and the audience you serve. Find the content holes—and fill them.

Chapter 25
The Influence Pyramid

Diving Into Your Fractals

Fractal marketing gets you to the point at which you can begin to tap into the community. But understanding *what* and *who* influences your chosen audience will give you more practical insight into how the community works. To do this, you have to understand the influence pyramid.

Before I break down the inner-workings of fractal marketing, let me introduce you to Vooray, a small, Utah-based apparel company that has leveraged the influence pyramid to sell hoodies, shirts, swimsuits, jackets, and hats.

The Human Slingshot and Board Shorts

Todd Nyman, Vooray's president, describes the Vooray clothing line as a lifestyle brand, summed up by its tagline, *Live. Ride. Play.* Vooray is a young company—it's only been around since 2010—and it doesn't have millions of dollars to invest in traditional marketing.

"We're young and we may be very small, but we've found a way to make ourselves relevant to all the kids that want to be part of the 'next big thing,'" Todd says.

Vooray was going after a very specific audience—one that spent time on YouTube looking for ways to live life to the fullest. Here's a flavor of the Vooray brand, and the audience they're targeting, right from the Vooray website:

> *"We LIVE to enjoy every minute of life. We RIDE, run, swim, work, jump, surf, bike, and whatever else, because we love when our hearts beat just a little faster. We PLAY because you can't take yourself too seriously after you work so hard to get there. Life is too short not to have fun every second."*

Rather than spend money on Google and Facebook ads, Todd's marketing team decided to hold events as marketing vehicles to promote their products. Todd wanted to get close to his customers and help them "live, ride, and play." And then he met Devin Graham.

Remember Devin—the filmmaker you met in Chapter 20 who makes extreme music videos? Well, Devin's also a Vooray customer. During the summer of 2011, Devin reached out to Todd Nyman at Vooray. From the get go, it was clear that Devin and Vooray shared the same values.

As Todd and Devin discussed ways they could work together, they hit on an idea. Why not leverage one of Vooray's extreme events to create some content for Devin to shoot? They'd both win. Vooray would get an awesome video and Devin would showcase his skills on his YouTube channel. Together, they could both drive viewers to the content.

Todd and his team set out to create an unparalleled experience. They wanted to show the world something that had never been seen before. Todd invited an exclusive list of Vooray VIPs to a little lake in Paradise, Utah. On the edge of the lake, the Vooray event staff built an incredible slip-and-slide that ended at an 8-foot tall ramp. The VIPs were invited to hold onto an inner-tube attached to a giant bungee cord, which in turn was pulled by a four-wheeler down the slide. The inner-tube would careen down the slip-and-slide, fly off the ramp, and fling the rider 120 feet into the air before splashing into the pristine pond. (If that description was too much for you to handle, check out Devin's video http://bit.ly/voorayanddevin).

Three days after the event, Devin had edited the video, set it to music, and posted it on his YouTube channel with an intriguing title: "Human Slingshot Slip-and-Slide." Within a few weeks, 2.5 million people had watched it. Who was watching it? Males between the ages of 18 and 44—exactly the demographic Vooray was looking to target. Sure, 172,000 people saw it on Facebook. Another 105,000 watched the video when it was featured on Gizmodo (a gadget website). But interestingly enough, 100,000 people saw the video on a European social networking site called VK.com. With more than 100 million active users, VK.com led to lucrative new opportunities for Vooray.

"We have had an overwhelming response. As a result of working with Devin, we now have international distribution and we're working with more distributors to expand our presence," Todd says.

But the brandscape they created is not a one-way street. Devin's audience has also grown significantly as a result of the "Slingshot" video. It's great content. It's something most people have never seen before. Only by working together was this content even possible. Vooray brought its audience, their VIP talent, and their event creation skills to the table. Devin created a great video and shared it with his engaged audience. Neither one would be as successful on their own. This is a beautiful brandscape.

"Anytime we collaborate with Devin, we see a huge surge in demand for our products. His body of work has a huge following and we're honored to be a part of that brandscape," Todd adds.

Was there any particular reason why this brandscape was so successful? Let's take a look at both of these communities to see how they came together to build a success story.

Breaking Down an Influence Pyramid

Working together, Devin and Vooray leveraged the influence effect. An influential content creator, Devin worked with a group of Vooray VIPs to create a video that Devin's audience devoured, embraced, and shared. Vooray promoted and distributed the video to their loyal fans, and in the end, attracted a whole new audience of consumers to Vooray's clothing and Devin's content.

It sounds complicated, but any community—even your audience of customers, clients, prospects, and leads—can be easily understood if you apply the influence pyramid.

At the top of the influence pyramid sits your company, your content, and your brand. In this case, the brand sitting at the top is Vooray. It's extremely difficult for any brand—no matter how big, cool, or exciting—to be relevant to all customers all of the time. But there is a subset of customers, clients, leads, and prospects who *are* interested in your stuff more often than everyone else in the digital world. They are the *digital influencers*.

Devin Graham is a digital influencer. He's a loyal Vooray customer. He loves what they stand for and what they do. He follows them on Twitter and Facebook. But most importantly, he creates content on a frequent enough basis to have built an audience all his own. That's an important distinction. Devin Graham is only a digital influencer because his audience devours his content.

The next tier of the influence pyramid is what we call the *prosumers*. Vooray's VIPs and Devin's YouTube subscriber base would be considered prosumers. Typically, a prosumer is someone who writes reviews for your products, or the product category. They're the people who write reviews for everything they buy. They are digitally engaged consumers who make an effort to connect with the brands and content creators they adore, follow, fan, and friend. The only difference between a digital influencer and a prosumer is that prosumers don't have their own content platforms. They engage on the platforms of others.

Prosumers are unbelievably powerful. These are the people who influence consumer decisions. If you're the cool kid in school, you're a prosumer. Everyone's looking to you for what's next. They're looking to you for the cool content. In order to authentically tap into this audience, you must build an authentic, trusted relationship with them.

Vooray's built a loyal audience of VIP customers. In fact, they've even monetized their VIP program to make sure that the customers who sign up for it value the access, invitations, and exclusive content that Vooray provides just to them. You can purchase a VIP membership on Vooray's website for three bucks a year. It's not a lot of money, but it's enough to ensure that the VIPs are committing to the brand. Vooray's VIP program supplied all the people who appeared in Devin's video. Vooray harnessed the power of their prosumer base.

Devin's audience is largely made up of prosumers who engage heavily on YouTube. They're males, between the ages of 18 and 44, who love the lifestyle content that Devin creates. They subscribe to his channel, get notified when he uploads a new video (every Tuesday), and, if they like it, they're the ones who share it with their friends—their friends on

Facebook, their YouTube connections, and their Twitter followers. Devin's and Vooray's prosumers helped make and elevate the content they created.

Finally, at the bottom tier of the influence pyramid is the consumer—everyone else you're trying to reach. It's the rest of the world. It's your target market. It's the prosumers of other brands. The vast majority of your new business comes out of the bottom of the pyramid.

BRAND INFLUENCE PYRAMID

Figure 6: Influencers lead, prosumers seed, and consumers read.

Think of it this way: Digital influencers "lead" the conversation by creating content their audience finds valuable. Prosumers "seed" the conversation by asking questions, soliciting suggestions, and sharing their insight. Consumers "read" the content, watch the videos, even peruse the comments, but they don't necessarily build a long-term relationship with your brand, the content, or even the digital influencer.

Remember it like this: *Influencers lead, prosumers seed,* and *consumers read.*

You can break down any community or audience by mapping out its influence pyramid—whether it's a Facebook group, a LinkedIn community, or even a YouTube channel. As a rule of thumb, only one percent of your total audience is likely to be considered digital influencers. Only six to nine percent will turn out to be prosumers. That means 90 percent of your audience can be influenced by seven to 10 percent of the consumers you're targeting.

Joining audiences by working with digital influencers to create content that authentically engages prosumers is perfect brandscaping. The prosumers help spread the word and build momentum for the content you've created together. It's a win-win.

Ironically, the bigger your company is, the harder it is to narrow down your most valuable audiences. In effect, you need to think like a focused, small-business owner to define your audience. You need to think like Todd Nyman at a growing startup with a small marketing budget.

Thinking Long Term

As of July 2012, Devin's video had been viewed nearly 7.7 million times. Vooray's still reaping the benefits from this authentic partnership. They've created a few more videos together, including an extreme mudfight and an aerial bicycle show, and they have a few more in the works.

Devin and Todd are committed to working together for the long term. As Todd says, "Our style is very much embodied in the videos Devin has created with us. We're helping grow each other's brands and businesses. We're both realizing our dreams together."

This is exactly the right kind of attitude for a brandscaper to have. Both parties must think about long-term, mutually beneficial relationships. They must leverage their resources to help each other grow. They have to embrace their shared values and focus on the audiences they already have.

WHAT IF...

You may already be aware that there's a duct tape craft revolution sweeping the United States. If you're not, you probably don't have a teenage female living in your house. Around the country, kids (and even some adults) have used regular old duct tape to create functional fashion accessories like wallets, rings, roses, necklaces, bracelets, broaches, flip-flops, and even purses. Duct tape crafts are a trend, a movement, ready to be embraced.

One of the most logical brands to have harnessed the power of this trend are the duct tape manufacturers themselves. Duck Tape Brand Duct Tape (that's a mouthful) has taken it upon themselves to create an entire website dedicated to teaching people how to make these fun items. Obviously, the more people they encourage to take on this hobby, the more tape they'll sell.

ShurTech Brands, the company that makes Duck Tape, partnered with a crafty website called MonkeySee.com where they've produced a series of over-produced, inauthentic, tutorials hosted by "Kristy from Duck Brand." (It's a great attempt at a brandscape, but it lacks authentic talent.)

What if, instead of using their own branded "expert," ShurTech invested in helping a digital influencer create authentic content for his or her existing audience?

It doesn't take much time to find a duct tape craft influencer on YouTube. Sarah Lynn, better known as SoCraftastic online, has created one of the most watched duct tape wallet tutorials on the web. But she's also created tons of other craft tutorials for her 59,000 YouTube subscribers. She has an avid and engaged crafting audience and I'm willing to bet she inspires a lot of people to purchase crafting wares.

Sarah Lynn's channel "…is devoted to all things artsy, crafty, recycled, fun, and cute," and as of July 2012 her video tutorials had garnered nearly 10 million views. Her army of prosumers has left 3,300 comments on her most popular video, which has been watched nearly 1.2 million times.

What if ShurTech embraced Sarah Lynn's tutorials and her audience of prosumers and consumers? What if ShurTech partnered with Michaels Arts and Crafts (where Sarah Lynn shops) to help drive in-store traffic by leveraging her talents? What if Sarah Lynn embarked on a nationwide Duck Tape tutorial tour hosted at Michaels Stores around the country?

I guarantee Sarah Lynn's videos, her bubbly personality, and the rabid fan base she's built would have been a better investment than Michaels' YouTube video tutorial on how to create a duct tape journal cover.

What if you looked for the Sarah Lynn in your industry?

Ask Yourself...

How do we quantify the value of a digital influencer's audience?

This is a great question to ask as we dissect your fractals and build influence pyramids. The problem is, you really won't know until you try embracing the influencer's audience and fueling his or her passion (and, as a result, inspire his or her prosumers to take action).

The quality of the relationships you build in the influencer pyramid will depend on the influencer's credibility and the level of trust he or she has built with the prosumers who consume their content. As a brand with a vested interest, you're going to have to build a minor league of digital talent and evaluate each influencer against the others.

Is Sarah Lynn (SoCraftastic) more effective at driving demand than ShurTech's own corporate spokesperson distributing videos on MonkeySee? Not if you're buying eyeballs and impressions, but I guarantee that over a few videos Sarah will win the day.

Remember, you're creating content as an asset, not an expense. Will your money be better spent fueling someone who's already passionate about your product and what it can do—or buying eyeballs for a corporate video?

Chapter 26
Align Around Common Values

What Do You Believe In?

So far, I've shown you how to form the right kind of content-based, audience-first partnerships. I've shown you how to identify niche audiences, find the content holes in their universes, and partner with influencers who already reach those markets. But what about your core values? What do you stand for? What about you is really going to make others trust you?

Your core values aren't emblazoned on your website. They're probably not in your tag line (although they may be). Values are not the features and functions your product delivers or the type of service you provide. You need to dig really deep to understand where your audience and your values collide. Vooray's "live, ride, play" is an easy example. But what about a B2B company that sells software as a service (SaaS)?

Do You Workshift?

Citrix Online is the parent company behind GoToMeeting, GoToMyPC, GoToWebinar, GoToTraining, and a slew of other SaaS products. You've probably been exposed to GoToMeeting on a webinar or a sales pitch.

Quite simply, GoToMeeting allows anyone to host an online meeting from his or her computer, enabling them to share their desktop applications with up to 15 attendees in real time. Each of Citrix Online's products has its own product pitch. For example, GoToMyPC allows users to securely access their desktop Mac or PC from the web. GoToTraining allows companies to train customers or employees without traveling.

But what's the core value underneath these? What could the parent brand do to help acquire customers for any of their diverse products? What makes Citrix Online unique in the market? What's the one thing that differentiates all these individual products? What's Citrix Online's core value?

While each product in their solution set has any number of competitors (FuzeMeeting competes directly with GoToMeeting, for example), no one is better positioned to help businesses work with anyone from anywhere for a wide variety of needs. From online training to online meetings, creating digital screencasts, or delivering online support, Citrix's entire product set supports its position in the market.

So, Citrix Online's core values might be expressed like this: "Citrix Online provides businesses of every size with the tools they need to work with anyone from anywhere."

Compare my core value statement to this one from their website's "About Us" page: Citrix Online tools allow customers "to work from anywhere with anyone—using our remote-connectivity and online collaboration solutions to save time, get more done, and connect to others around the world."

There's nothing wrong with the statement above—it's a great positioning statement. But if you're going to successfully brandscape, your core values must be consumer-focused—not product-focused.

In 2009, Citrix Online embraced the idea of building a brandscape. They wanted to tap into a trend and build a movement—a movement designed to encourage employees to work from remote offices, a movement that built confidence in an employee's ability to stay connected no matter where he or she worked. They envisioned a brandscape that would leverage well-known digital influencers who are constantly on the road and have lessons and insight to share.

One of the digital influencers Citrix embraced to help build this project was best-selling author, frequent business traveler, and prolific blogger, Chris Brogan, president of Human Business Works. "As more and more companies look for ways to give their employees flexibility in their working environments and situations, helping people perform remote functions is a must," Chris says.

Obviously, if the brandscaping strategy was successful, Citrix would increase demand for its products, as well as its competitors' products.

But they'd benefit from being part of the movement, instead of the trailing end of a trend.

Chris and the Citrix Online team coined a new term designed to encapsulate their core values: *workshifting.*

Citrix launched an online platform at Workshifting.com that's designed to help employees and employers explore the challenges and opportunities presented by a remote workforce. As their site explains:

> *"If you work out of coffee shops, hotels, airports, and your home every bit as much as you do in the office, Workshifting.com is for you. We share resources on telecommuting, online tools, travel, technology, business, and virtual offices to help you shift when, where, and how you work."*

Very little of the content on Workshifting.com promotes or explicitly endorses Citrix's product offerings; in fact, the content covers a wide variety of topics.

What's even more impressive is that the majority of the content on Workshifting.com is written by 32 digital influencers. As contributors who frequently work from non-traditional offices, these bloggers create relevant content. They share it with their audiences and constantly grow exposure for the concept of workshifting.

It wasn't easy finding the best, most relevant, digital influencers. "We sought out bloggers and content creators who had dual lives—online social media types who also were employed by mid- to large-size corporations. This is a tricky audience to find, but we found that they self-identified, more than anyone else," Chris says.

The content these bloggers create covers everything from how to better manage your time when you're working from home, to ensuring that you retain your professionalism even though you're still in your pajamas.

In one article, "7 Considerations for Setting Up a Home Office," written by Sharlyn Lauby, one of the top bloggers in the HR industry, the content even touts the benefits of tools that could be considered eventual competitors of Citrix Online, like Google Voice.[32]

Workshifting, as a movement, has become fairly widespread since Citrix began promoting the concept in 2009. Even a quick Google search reveals that there are more than 117,000 results referencing the term, including media brands such as *Businessweek*, *ZDNet*, and *WE Magazine*.

Has it worked? Absolutely. So much so that Citrix has created a "Global Workshifting Index." Its most recent results indicate that by the end of 2013, 93 percent of organizations will have implemented formal workshifting policies, representing an increase of more than 45 percent from 2012.[33]

Workshifting.com is the embodiment of a clearly executed brandscape—one that Citrix was able to develop once it defined and embraced core values. Citrix then partnered with influential content creators to create a movement that's become part of the corporate lexicon. Do you workshift?

Articulate Your Core Values

Whether you're a B2B brand, like Citrix Online, or a consumer packaged goods company, a clearly articulated core value statement will set the foundation for successful brandscape partnerships by explaining why others should align with you. It also helps you focus on what types of people and brands to align with.

It's never too soon to create a core value statement. It doesn't have to be perfect, but it must be unique. As you begin exploring the content your audience consumes, you may have to adjust it anyway to ensure that you're providing consumers with something no other brand can—even when it comes to the type of content you create, distribute, and promote.

Converse "believes that unleashing the creative spirit will change the world"—that's what Converse's CMO, Jeff Cottrill, believes is the company's core value.[34] That's why Converse built a music studio. That's why they've embraced the arts. Converse's core value doesn't say anything about shoes.

There are only three rules for creating a workable value statement:

1. It must be unique. There's a tendency for companies to say things like "it's our people that make us unique." While this might be true, any other company in the world can say this and maintain that it's true. Your people may make your brand unique, but how?

2. It must be consumer-focused. Think like the customer when you're verbalizing your core values. Ask yourself what makes your company unique from the customer's perspective. Saying your proprietary technology makes you unique doesn't mean anything to the consumer.

3. It must be reflected in everything you do. Dig deep to find something that is at the core of what you do or what you make. Constantly ask yourself and your team why you do what you do. Keep asking until you just can't ask anymore.

To help you get started, consider this core value statement I created for Nordstrom: "At Nordstrom, we forge long-term relationships with each customer we serve by providing personal shopping advice that fits your lifestyle."

For years, Nordstrom has been touted as a department store brand with exceptional customer service. But just saying you have exceptional customer service isn't enough. That's not unique enough in the marketplace. Nordstrom staff members are lifestyle advisors, not just sales associates. That's unique. It's at the core of what they do.

Crafting a good value statement is more about making sure you understand what it's *not*, than what it *is*. Here are a few things to avoid when writing yours:

- Don't use industry jargon or double-speak. Get rid of the gobbledygook.
- Don't overcomplicate the value you provide in the market.
- Avoid expressing what *you* think is unique about your company, and work to explore what your customers, clients, and even your competitors believe is unique.
- Don't overlook your competition (or even your perceived competition) in the marketplace. Sometimes, understanding your competitor's values can help you define and eliminate things you think might be unique about your company.

- Never discredit what the media, bloggers, competitors, or even Facebook users say about your brand. Sometimes, reviewing what's being said about you in the marketplace can help uncover things you take for granted that actually define your brand in the minds of the consumers in your market.

As Citrix Online demonstrated with Workshifting.com, a clearly articulated value statement will define your brand in a crowded marketplace.

WHAT IF...

As a frequent business traveler, I've done my fair share of workshifting. I've camped out at many a Starbucks to get work done in between business meetings. I've used their WiFi to attend webinars and pitched clients from their comfy chairs while on my cell phone.

What if Starbucks actually embraced the workshifting community? What if they created workshifting-reserved tables at their shops? I always like a table close to an outlet, away from the door. What if Citrix actually worked with Starbucks to brand these tables, or to provide workshifting customers with advice on how to work better in a busy store?

What if hotels had workshifting rooms? I always find myself needing a later checkout, more outlets, and a more practical desk than most hotels provide. I can honestly say, if a hotel brand offered a special workshifting membership, with rooms and services designed for a frequent business traveler like me, I'd be a loyal customer (I'd even pay to be part of that club). Wouldn't you?

Let me be clear: this doesn't have to cost a lot of money, or any money at all. Workshifting is an idea Starbucks and hotel chains should (and could) embrace for free today. What if Citrix helped other brands understand that embracing, marketing, and communicating around the same core values will drive new—and more valuable—customers to their coffee shops and hotels?

Ask Yourself...

What is our core value statement?

Don't let your mission statement on the plaque in the lobby suffice for your core value statement. Take some time (just a few hours) to define a message that will clearly convey what you stand for and what you believe in, specifically for your brandscaping effort.

This exercise isn't easy, and it's even more difficult if you try to go it alone. The best way to get to a working value statement quickly is to gather no more than 10 people from your senior leadership team in one room for four hours. Explicitly set the goal of arriving at a working value statement at the outset, and manage your time wisely. Use the entire four hours, even if you think you have a unique value statement half-way through.

As the facilitator, you must constantly challenge the team to question whether the statement you've written is consumer-focused, truly unique in the marketplace, and embodies everything you do. If you get stuck, bring up a competitor's website and define *their* core value, then review your working statement to see if it still rings true.

If your statement seems vague, or has too many words in it, start editing. Eliminate words that don't mean anything, or words that your competition already uses. Remember, a good core value statement is simple.

Review your final statement at the beginning of each marketing meeting for the next six weeks. It will evolve, even after your first meeting, but make sure the entire team understands the ultimate message you want to communicate to potential brandscaping partners.

Chapter 27
Don't Publish, Underwrite

The Content Bubble

There's a content bubble and it's going to burst—and I'm not the only one who thinks so.

"I do think we're in the early stages of a content bubble, which is being inflated by the idea that brands should be publishers," said Kyle Monson, content-strategy director at JWT, New York, in a recent *Ad Age* article.[35]

The fact is, corporations shouldn't try to become media companies. You shouldn't decide that in addition to running a restaurant, manufacturing a product, or selling consulting services that you're going to become a media brand. The media industry is in flux. Even the best media companies in the world can't figure out how to be good, profitable publishers. You need to avoid the temptation to become a media company.

And quite frankly, most of you are really crappy media companies. "There are a few really great content campaigns out there, and loads of terrible ones," Monson went on to observe in the *Ad Age* piece. "The balance is such that, eventually, CMOs might not want to hear about clever content campaigns anymore, because they've traveled that road before and didn't see the ROI. That's how bubbles pop."

You run a company. You sell stuff. You're not a publisher. Don't try to be one. Instead, you need to focus on forcing media companies to give you what you need. You don't need impressions and eyeballs from ads—just say no. You don't need one-hit wonders from PR firms. Tell your PR partners you want more than a giant number of impressions. You don't need celebrity endorsements; you need authentic, long-term relationships with content creators who believe in the same things you do. You don't need anymore one-night stands; you need a series of marketing marriages designed to increase demand for whatever you sell.

The content marketing fervor has created lots of interest, hype, and excitement around how effective valuable content can be. That, I completely agree with. But, instead of looking to create the content yourself, like a media company, partner with talent that's already doing it. Find brands that are creating something of value. Pool your resources with others and share your audience. Become a brandscaper instead of a publisher.

Campaign-thinking won't deliver the ROI you're expecting. If you're looking at content as a marketing expense instead of a corporate asset, you'll never justify the expense. Good content isn't cheap.

You need to think more like public broadcasting than a media company. You need to think about underwriting valuable content that drives new business instead of advertising, endorsements, sponsorships, or plain old PR.

The Concept of Underwriting

Marketers love to sponsor stuff. We love to sponsor sporting events, entertainment venues, and nonprofits. We adore seeing our logo on signs at trade shows (the bigger the better). We love to raise awareness of our brand by attaching it to things people actually pay attention to.

By definition, a sponsorship is "a cash or in-kind fee paid to a property in return for access to the exploitable commercial potential associated with that property."[36]

A sponsorship is not a partnership. "Exploiting" another's brand for the benefit of yours isn't mutually symbiotic. Instead, sponsors are parasites feeding off the value of another's brand and the content it creates. Sponsoring something may raise awareness for your brand, but in what context? Sponsorships are superficial, temporary brand relationships.

Underwriting is different. Underwriting is a true partnership between a content brand and a company that believes in the value of the content being created. The Public Broadcasting Service (PBS) and National Public Radio (NPR) leverage the concept of underwriting to ensure that individual programming can be funded and produced.

For example, Sprint is an underwriter of the PBS series *NOVA*.

"Communication, technology, and science are intertwined. That's why Sprint proudly sponsors NOVA on PBS to help bring this informative public television series into the homes of millions of Americans. We are pleased to congratulate NOVA for remaining at the forefront of our high-tech world, educating and inspiring viewers for 30 years."[37]

Sprint's underwriting message connects the dots between Sprint's core values, *NOVA's* programming, and the audience it serves. Google also underwrites *NOVA*, but for different reasons:

"At Google we value above all else the curious mind—the driving force behind so many advances in science and technology. For 30 years *NOVA* on PBS has embodied these values, presenting programming that encourages millions of viewers to ponder new possibilities. We are grateful for, and are proud to support, *NOVA's* commitment to scientific exploration, and we look forward to the new discoveries we expect it to inspire."[38]

Together, Sprint and Google have created a brandscape. Some might even consider Sprint and Google competitors (Google does sell cell phones), but they both value the content *NOVA* creates and they've brought together their brands to help ensure PBS continues to "inspire" and "educate" viewers that both brands want to touch.

At such a large scale and with such a broad audience, Google and Sprint's underwriting of *NOVA* doesn't sound like it will increase demand for the products they sell (and it probably doesn't directly correlate). But that doesn't mean underwriting won't be effective at a more focused, fractal level.

The PBS Rule Book

Interestingly enough, tucked away on a webpage on the PBS website, you'll find its "Funding Standards & Practices." In a section titled "How to create PBS underwriting messages," you'll find six rules for creating a message that would air on any of its programming.

Coincidentally enough, these rules sound like basic content marketing rules. Here they are:

Avoid the following elements:

1. Calls to action
2. Price or value information
3. Superlative descriptions or qualitative claims
4. Direct comparisons with other companies, their products, or services
5. Inducements to purchase (like a promotion)
6. Endorsements.

Whether they knew it or not, all the people and brands we've looked at in this book all followed PBS' rules for creating a message. Bank of America helped underwrite *The Story of Us*. Vooray helped underwrite Devin Graham's YouTube videos. Advertisers helped underwrite *Brew Masters*. Indium underwrote the content of its internal experts, while Swarovski and London Jewelers both got behind *JCK Rock Star*. Underwriting, not advertising, is the future of all marketing.

The Stuff of Legends

Iconic sunglass manufacturer Ray-Ban celebrated its 75th anniversary in 2012. They've put lots of marketing muscle behind the celebration and accompanying advertising campaign. They've created award-winning advertisements and an interactive Facebook app. They've built an interactive, digital timeline featuring a series of celebrity-inspired stories exploring the heritage of their brand. They're even inviting consumers to upload their own stories leveraging their campaign tag line: "Never Hide." This is very traditional stuff, with one exception: they're brandscaping with the A.V. Club.

The A.V. Club (AVClub.com) is an entertainment-oriented website and newspaper that serves up a healthy dose of pop culture content to 6 million consumers a month. In 2011, they began producing a video program called *Pop Pilgrim: A Travel Show for the Pop Culture Enthusiast*. As they say in the intro, "When the A.V. Club travels we always make time to visit pop culture landmarks. If something memorable happened in the world of film, television, books, or music, we want to go there. We're not just tourists. *We're Pop Pilgrims*." And travel they do.

In one episode, they visited the Houston private school featured in the movie *Rushmore.* They've gone to the Georgia locations featured on the cover of R.E.M. albums and the Pennsylvania cemetery from *Night of the Living Dead.* Over the course of the existing 33 episodes, they've entertained their audience by telling the stories behind numerous locations, people, and events. They've uncovered the inspiration for legendary locations, imagery, films, and music.

Ray-Ban and the A.V. Club are targeting the same audience. They're both interested in telling stories that have defined the last 75 years of pop culture. The A.V. Club needs to fund and finance their high-quality, frequently delivered content targeted at a well-defined niche audience—the same audience Ray-Ban wants to reach with its Legends Collection of iconic eyewear. This is a perfect brandscape.

Every episode of *Pop Pilgrims* is underwritten by Ray-Ban. The show's introductory animation reads, "Presented by Ray-Ban, genuine since 1937." The web page is wrapped with Ray-Ban branding and messaging supporting the show's message.

Ray-Ban is supporting the creation of valuable content in the same way that Exxon Mobil, Sprint, and Google support *NOVA.* Together, Ray-Ban and the A.V. Club are following PBS' rules for underwriting. This is the future of all advertising—underwriting.

Underwriting in the Future

In the future, we'll see more "brought to you by," and less "sponsored by." We'll see more "supported by," and less "endorsed by."

Moving forward, brands will need to attach their companies to content in a more meaningful way. You should be the brand that brings me the content that I need. You should be the company that supports the content creators I value and have a relationship with. Instead of trying to be a valuable content creator yourself, align your company with the ones already out there.

If you're a hardware store, start writing about backyard poultry or forge a relationship with someone like the Chicken Whisperer to help him or her achieve greater reach.

If you're Breville and you want to sell more panini presses, hire someone to create hundreds of panini recipes or underwrite the Panini Happy blog for the next 10 years.

If you're a clothing retailer, build a content marketing strategy dishing out fashion advice on your own website or find someone else already doing so on YouTube and underwrite his or her content.

If you sell automotive parts to industry manufacturers, stop trying to sell the virtue of your features and functions and help content creators who target car designers and automotive engineers.

If you're a medical device manufacturer, stop trying to convince the media to pick-up your story and start working with other brands that target your buyers to create content that helps medical personnel do their jobs more efficiently.

If you own a restaurant, what have you done to increase the number of people who come to your area to shop, eat, relax, and be entertained? Find the digital influencers already promoting your area and ask them what you can do to increase the quality of their content.

I could go on and on with examples from any industry for any audience (take that as a challenge). There are people out there creating great content for just about every subject under the sun. Go find them and help them create a hook, build a format, increase their frequency, and expand their reach.

WHAT IF...

You don't have to consider underwriting content a purely financial investment. Any of your resources can be leveraged to inspire and engage the content creators you're looking to attract.

At bars and comedy clubs around the world, open mic nights have provided comedians with an opportunity to practice their craft. These establishments don't host open mic nights because they are feeling charitable. They host these events to bring in patrons on traditionally slow nights.

What if you were one of these establishments and you invited the entire world in to watch the show live? What if you helped the comedians record and distribute their content? What if you leveraged your physical assets to encourage the creation of great content right from your very own place of business?

The Waffle Shop in Pittsburgh does exactly that. In the middle of the restaurant, they've built a stage, set up a few cameras, and broadcast a live-streaming talk show with their customers. Sure, they sell waffles from 11 p.m. to 3 a.m. every Friday and Saturday night. But they also shoot a live talk show in the middle of the restaurant, and the restaurant is packed!

The Waffle Shop's programming line-up includes three shows: *Open Talk*, *Cookspeak*, and *Waffle Wopp*. Each has its own format. *Open Talk* invites anyone (and they do mean anyone) to step up to the stage and talk about anything (and they do mean anything). *Cookspeak* features Tom Totin, a local Pittsburgh cook, delivering "out of the box" culinary commentary. *Waffle Wopp* is a magazine talk show hosted and produced by Pittsburgh teenagers—its eclectic guest list, live music, and fun interviews make it The Waffle Shop's most popular show.

The Waffle Shop doesn't create the content that fills their restaurant each weekend, they only provide the resources to empower content creators to practice their craft, share their stories, and create, distribute, and amplify the results. The Waffle Shop underwrites the creation of content.

Interestingly, there's an additional layer of context (and content) behind The Waffle Shop: it actually functions as a real-world classroom for students from Carnegie Mellon University (CMU). It's an "eatery, a television production studio, a social catalyst, and a business."[39]

CMU professor Jon Rubin is the mastermind behind this giant content experiment. "The students get to try out their ideas in the real world," he says. "The classroom is the real world. Our critics are our customers." The class, which is offered by the school's art program, invites students to "create a cultural experience that adds something unique to the city."[40]

CMU is underwriting The Waffle Shop, which in turn, is underwriting the creation of community-driven content.

What if *you* pooled your resources with a local educational institution and invited the community to create content with you? What if you started to underwrite great content instead of just advertise in it?

Ask Yourself...

Where should we invest our underwriting dollars?

You've got lists of things you need to *stop* doing and lists of things you need to *start* doing. You've got market analyses to back up the trends that move your market and a list of content creators who have embraced those trends (and you know who hasn't). You've analyzed your fractals and identified the content holes.

You've taken the time to consume your audience's content. You've set expectations with your audience and set an appointment with them. You've worked with other brands to craft a hook, build a format, and brand your content. (Or maybe you've created more than one.)

Where should you invest your underwriting dollars? You tell me. Who shares the same values as your brand? Who has the most powerful prosumer audience? Which brands are closest to defining the need for your products?

Brandscaping is part science and part art, but it's a methodology that works. Get off the sidelines and invest in a content asset that has the potential to grow your business beyond your wildest dreams. Stop marketing and start brandscaping.

Conclusion
Start Small, Think Big

Pool Your Resources

We live in a resource-strapped world. No marketer I know has
enough money, staff, time, and energy to keep up with every new
media channel, their advertising agency, or even their expense
reports—let alone find new resources to tweet, update their status on
Facebook, or review the latest PowerPoint deck. It's not going to get
any easier to keep up with every new content demand in the
marketplace. The solution is to pool our resources.

First off, conduct a resource audit in your organization. A resource is
anything from which benefit can be produced. Obviously, your
organization has some money if you have revenue—*money* is a
resource. You have *internal* resources, like the people who staff your call
center, wait tables at your restaurant, or consult with your clients. You
have *intellectual* resources, like the studies you've done in the
marketplace or product research you've undertaken with your best
customers. You have *facilities,* whether it's a restaurant, a shoe store, a
rock-climbing wall, a video studio, or a bunch of computers—these are
all viable resources to leverage in your brandscaping plan.

You also probably have a wealth of *intellectual capital* that's never
been written down, captured in a PowerPoint presentation, or even
videotaped for internal use. The knowledge your team has—the
expertise and insight they have accrued over years and years of
experience—is extremely valuable. Too often, I see companies trying to
manufacture inauthentic ads, "funny viral video concepts," and
feature-driven press releases, only to find that the best stories, the deep
market insight, and the rich, compelling content has been overlooked
and dismissed.

Sit down with people in your organization so you can uncover the
intellectual capital that they have about your business, your customers,

your partners, and even your vendors. It's called *intellectual capital* because it's valuable. It's an asset waiting to be leveraged with other partners in your brandscape.

Another valuable resource is your *audience*. It's valuable to content creators who are trying to grow the number of people they reach. It's valuable to other brands that would love to have access to the audience you already serve. It's probably safe to say that your audience is the most underutilized resource in your organization. It's also one you've probably never considered leveraging as a marketing asset.

Partnerships Build Audiences

Danny Bennett intrinsically understood and leveraged the power of Tony Bennett's brand with people who trusted and respected Tony's reputation and legendary status in the music business to create content that reached an entirely new audience—and he didn't have to spend a dime to do it.

Each pop icon who sang a duet with Tony was telling the world how much he or she loved his music, and the results were phenomenal. The easy-to-understand exponential audience growth that resulted is something all marketers can achieve if they look for content partners their audience is already engaged with.

In the new media world, finding your own content partners will not only create a powerful and endless supply of great content, but also expose your brand, products, and services to their audiences. You no longer need the distribution channels of old (mass media) to expose yourself to a new audience. All you need is a partner with an email distribution list, a Facebook fan page, or a bunch of followers on Twitter or YouTube.

Are You Ready to Brandscape?

Brandscaping is a big idea. It's a way of thinking. It's not for everyone.

Brandscaping is NOT for...

- Lazy marketers looking to inflate their Facebook fans by offering promotions, freebies, or discounts.
- Social media wannabes who believe that engagement at all costs is more important than the value of interaction.
- SEO gurus who think gaming the system will generate quality customer leads.
- Corporate big wigs who think they know better than authentic talent with a trusting audience.
- PR professionals who love the allure of traditional media more than the value of new niches.
- Advertising executives who want to create sexy campaigns, build microsites, and spend media dollars to win awards.
- Brands that believe they can create better content than anyone else in the market.

Brandscaping IS for...

- Brands that speak to real people, not faceless customers.
- Those who see the value of other people's audiences—and the power of sharing their own.
- Executives who are humble enough to believe that their customers purchase more than just their brand.
- Companies that are willing to support talent (no matter how small) that's having an impact on their business.
- People who believe that pooling their resources will make their budgets go farther.

Brandscaping isn't for everyone. But, is it for you?

As You Move Through Your Brandscaping Journey…

There are a lot of ideas in this book—too many to tackle at once. So start small, but think big. Here are some thoughts I'll leave you with:

- The more you embrace fractal marketing, the more opportunities you'll find.
- Surf the web like Galileo, and the less you'll feel like Ptolemy.
- Question every ad exec, media partner, and PR person.
- Stop contributing to information overload.
- Value quality over quantity.
- Embrace everyone's audience and their existing brandscapes.
- Look for talent and keep searching for the next big thing.
- Build a content brand instead of creating branded content.
- Start with Twitter, but dream of TV.
- Treat your content as an asset.
- Build a format and create a hook.
- Start a movement…tap into a trend.
- Find the content holes.
- Embrace the influencers, listen to the prosumers, and reach the consumers.
- Focus on your core values.
- Don't try to do everything at once.
- Don't try to be everything to everyone.
- Pick one audience.
- Find brandscape partners whose values align with yours.
- Build one success story.
- Then start again.
- Be a brandscaper.

Appendix
Brandscaping Extended

Brandscaping is an idea, a concept, a methodology; it enables you to leverage your resources to extend your reach, relevance, and relationships. It's a flexible concept that can be applied to everything from designing your next product to launching a startup.

Your ability to extend the idea of brandscaping to any aspect of your business is only as limited as your imagination.

Here you'll find just a few examples of how thinking like a brandscaper can transform your business. If you're considering building an app, wish you worked for a startup, love a specific band, want to save your publishing business, or want to make the world a better place, these examples are for you.

Appendix 1
Brandscape to Create an App

Build It, Buy It, or Brand It

Everyone's hot for apps today. The problem is, you're not an app developer (unless, of course, you're in the software business).

So, how do you go about getting one? There are three options:

- You can build it on your own—a good option if you have the staff, the desire to commit to the process, and the patience to see it to fruition.
- You can buy it from someone else—off the shelf "app builder" software will give consumers the appearance that you have an app. Or, you can hire a developer to build the exact app you think your consumers want. The problem with this approach, however, is that game-changing ideas don't come from you and your team designing an app. They come from innovative thinkers who believe they have a new idea.
- Which leads me to the third option—look for someone with a great idea. Trust me, there is already someone out there building a really great app that your audience would love. All you need to do is brand it.

The fact is, there are startups out there who are faster than you, more nimble than you, and more well-equipped than you to build apps. The problem they face is a lack of resources. That's where you come in. What can you offer? Money? Data? Access to partners, business advice, or maybe just office space with a phone, printer, and an Internet connection?

I happen to know someone who fueled his startup by brandscaping an app. Here's his story.

Zazu and the Morning Report

In 2009, I had the pleasure of working with an intern at my marketing agency named Marc Held. Marc was a senior in high school at the time, but it was clear to me, and everyone who met him, that Marc would go places. He spent a year at Tippingpoint Labs before heading off to Northeastern University for his freshman year.

While at school Marc had an idea. Every morning he was jarred awake by his cell phone's alarm. He didn't use an old-fashioned desktop alarm clock, he just used his smartphone. But he realized his smartphone's alarm clock was pretty dumb. Why couldn't his smartphone engage him in the morning? All his smartphone's alarm clock could do was beep, sing, or buzz. He thought, "There must be a better way. It's a smartphone, right?"

Immediately, he set about building what he called "the smartest damn alarm clock." Marc's Android app would actually help you get your day started, instead of just wake you up.

At the prescribed time, Zazu (as the app was named) would deliver personalized information to help you wake up. If you had an appointment in an hour, a computer voice would remind you that your meeting downtown starts in 50 minutes. It would then go on to read you some news stories from your favorite websites. It would tell you what the traffic was like for your trip downtown. It would even remind you to grab an umbrella before you left.

While you were getting ready in the morning, Zazu would help you get the information you needed without looking at a screen, touching buttons, or interrupting your routine. Essentially, Zazu would be a personalized alarm clock with a morning radio show designed just for you.

Marc's initial Android app held so much promise that he actually dropped out of college to pursue building the application full time. He built a small team of smart people to start hacking away at the app and they started looking for funding.

That's when he started brandscaping. Who wants to own your morning? Who wants to be as close as possible to the moment you wake up? You guessed it, cereal manufacturers. Marc's team won the opportunity to partner with The Quaker Oats Company as part of a program designed by PepsiCo (which owns Quaker).

PepsiCo10, as it's called, "matches technology, media, and communications entrepreneurs with PepsiCo brands to activate pilot programs in digital media and social marketing." Suddenly, Marc had access to the resources of one of the largest consumer goods manufacturers in the world.

"Zazu is a new opportunity for us to connect with our consumers when our products are most relevant to them," says Barbara Liss, director of digital for Quaker Oats. "For example, with Zazu, when a user wakes up to a snowy day with back-to-back meetings, we can share the idea to start their morning with the latest weather report and Instant Quaker Oatmeal, for a breakfast that will warm them up and help sustain them for their morning activities."[41]

Zazu also partnered with other brands including Samsung and Breville. Essentially, Quaker had helped fund Marc's startup. What did they get out of it? They found that contextual brand interactions, like the ones Zazu delivered, were eight times more effective than traditional advertisements. Quaker realized that owning the morning was possible and they didn't need to build an app to do it. All they had to do was contribute to Marc's success and brand it.

It's Not Easy

By 2012, Marc had moved on to a new full-time job. Zazu turned out to be a grand experiment. Somehow along the way, Marc's idea got bigger and bigger. Instead of just owning the morning, he wanted to own the whole day. Marc and his team shut the doors when they couldn't secure more funding.

The reality is, not every app is a winner. For all the apps in the app store, very few are gigantic mega hits. So instead of trying to build their own apps and keep up with the marketplace, smart brands like PepsiCo are doing what they can to help startups experiment, with the hope that one startup may become a breakout success.

This is a strategy almost any company can adopt. You don't have to be a Pepsi to offer up your office space in trade for some brand integration in a deep way—especially when it makes sense for your audience. It doesn't cost you anything to introduce your entire client base to an app you're helping develop. What does the app developer get out of it? Office space and an audience to adopt their invention. That's valuable.

It's time you and your team went to the app developer meet-ups in town. It's time you got your pulse on the smart little tech startups experimenting with big new ideas. You may be the connection they need between a good idea and a serviceable market.

If you want an app, remember, it's not easy, and you're not an app developer.

Appendix 2
Brandscape a Startup

Funding For a Reason

If you've ever doubted that it's possible to build an audience for a product before it's produced, spend some time on Kickstarter.com.

Kickstarter bills itself as a crowd-funding website for creative projects. Everything from indie film projects to video games and even iPod accessories have been pitched and fully funded (sometimes in days) by leveraging an audience of friends, family and followers pitching in. (I'm talking about funding that often hits $1 million, not fifty bucks.)

Sure, your next competitor might be trying to raise money on Kickstarter.com, but there may be opportunities for you to help a startup get exposure if your core values align. Thinking like a brandscaper opens you up to these types of new partnerships.

This is exactly what State Farm Insurance did in 2011 when it got behind an intriguing little startup.

State Farm & Soccer Balls

You've probably heard State Farm's core value and marketing message: "Like a good neighbor, State Farm is there." If you watch their advertising campaigns, you might start to think it's just an advertising slogan and not much more. But last year, State Farm did something special—something that indicates their slogan is more than just a catchy jingle. They helped a startup called Uncharted Play scale its business.

Hispanic-American consumers are an important market for State Farm, which sponsors a Latin American soccer championship called the Gold Cup. As part of their involvement with soccer, State Farm's advertising agency happened on a video demonstration of a device designed by four Harvard University students called the Soccket.

The Soccket is a soccer ball that generates electricity while it's being kicked. For every 15 minutes that kids (or adults for that matter) play with the ball, it provides three hours of power for a light that plugs into the ball. Twenty percent of the world's population doesn't have electricity, but a lot of those nations play soccer, even if the players have to use balled-up plastic bags.

State Farm loved the idea that being a good neighbor and a sponsor of a Latin American soccer tournament could mean more to their audience if they actually provided something of need to Latin American countries. So the marketing team reached out to Uncharted Play, the maker of the Soccket ball, to see what they could do.

Together, they hatched a plan. State Farm worked with its advertising agency to build an interactive game called "Play Today, Illuminate Tomorrow." The game launched on State Farm's Facebook page to 100,000 fans. Basically, the longer a game player kept a soccer ball in the air, the more "virtual" minutes of light he or she generated toward providing soccer balls to Latin American communities without electricity.

The goal was to generate 30,000 virtual minutes over the course of the entire Gold Cup tournament; however, within the first four days, more than 143,000 minutes had been logged and State Farm distributed 1,500 Soccket balls to countries in need.

Uncharted Play went from two full-time employees trying to keep their startup afloat, to seven staffers after State Farm purchased the balls—not to mention all the press coverage they received. The company is currently creating additional devices to plug into the Soccket balls, including an air purifier and a cell phone charger. And they're always looking for new partners.

As for State Farm, according to an *Ad Age* article, Hispanic insurance quotes and sales also spiked. It was a win-win.

Sounds like the makings of a beautiful brandscape, doesn't it? Well, unfortunately, that's the end of the story. The initiative was treated more like a campaign than a long-term relationship. After the Gold Cup in June 2011, State Farm took down the Facebook app. The microsite for the campaign is dead.

Marketers have to stop thinking like advertisers looking for the next big campaign. If State Farm truly wants to win the hearts and minds of Hispanic-American consumers, they need to *commit*. They need to commit not to 150,000 virtual minutes of electricity, but to a million minutes, or a billion minutes. They need to get in the game for the long haul.

How Can You Help a Startup Succeed?

Start looking for startups that are working on ideas that you, your customers, clients, and prospects could benefit from. Give them a call and ask them if there's anything you can do to help. I guarantee if you think long-term, it will pay off.

If you're a startup, look for opportunities to partner with brands that share your core values. Show them how a partnership with your start-up could make a difference in their bottom line and their brand image if they help you succeed.

Appendix 3
Brandscape to Music

Licensing Music Evolved

Like other forms of media, the music industry is in flux. Bands, musicians, and writers are faced with a paradoxical dilemma: it's never been easier to garner an audience, but it's never been harder to monetize their art. Many artists have turned to licensing their music to help subsidize their revenue.

Bands have partnered with advertising agencies to create music for commercials and advertisements in traditional-looking licensing partnerships. One of the most notable (and perhaps annoying) examples of this kind of licensing deal occurred during the holiday season of 2011, when Pomplamoose licensed their music (and their eclectic music stylings) to Hyundai (http://bit.ly/hyundaiholiday).

How can *you* take advantage of the many opportunities out there to help today's music acts get exposure? Here's how Devin Graham does it.

A Soundtrack for Your Brand

Remember Devin Graham? The extreme music video filmmaker you met earlier in the book? When I first saw Devin's JetLev water jet pack video on YouTube, I liked the song that accompanied the video. Devin included a link to download the song (*Get Lite*) on iTunes, so I downloaded it. I spent 99 cents on a song from a band I'd never heard of because I watched Devin's video. You can download it, too, if you want (http://bit.ly/GetLiteJetLev).

The song is the creation of a group called The Beatards, who had shot and uploaded their own music video for *Get Lite* almost a year before Devin created the JetLev video. After a year on YouTube, The Beatards video had less than 25,000 video views. Almost immediately after Devin released the water jet pack video, The Beatards video started to see an uptick in viewers. In the year since Devin's video hit the big time, The Beatards' video has been seen more than 100,000 times.

"There was a decent spike in sales for the song when the JetLev video hit," says Jesse Roman, the CEO of Step Up World, and the manager for The Beatards. The JetLev video didn't turn The Beatards into millionaires, but "it was a great avenue of exposure. Anytime you get your music in front of 5 million people, it translates into new fans and a growing fan base," Jesse adds.

Devin secured the rights to use *Get Lite* for free. (Devin does all the videos on his YouTube channel for free.) But imagine if Devin was actually driving his passion by brandscaping with video equipment manufacturers and had a music budget. Imagine if the Beatards promoted Devin's video as part of their promotional efforts in a deeper way. Imagine if Devin shot all their music videos?

The Beatards have a following, they have an audience, and they have fans. That audience is valuable.

The Beatards' primary source of revenue these days is licensing. Their music can be heard on tons of MTV shows and recently was featured on an episode of the television show *Glee*. They're doing well for themselves.

What up-and-coming band could become the soundtrack for your brand?

Exposing Your Audience to New Sounds

Music is a powerful media. It has the power to get stuck in the mind of the consumer. Every time I hear *Get Lite* on my iPod, I think of the JetLev R200. That's a powerful connection.

Musicians have the ability to attract a powerful, loyal, and personally connected fan base—one that any brand should be glad to be associated with. Instead of sponsoring an event, why not consider finding a soundtrack for your brand? Why not partner with a band that is authentically connected to the products and services you sell?

Every multimedia project is better with music. If you host a podcast, or produce videos, you'll need music that your audience identifies with. Instead of purchasing a cheesy, royalty-free music track, why not partner with an artist who's looking for exposure?

Appendix 4
Brandscape with Nonprofits

Aligning Core Values

Every company I've ever worked for donated money to a good cause at one time or another. I'm sure yours does, too.

Cash and event sponsorships are not the only resources you can donate. How about taking a brandscaper's approach to making a big impact in a charity your consumers care about?

Your audience is a resource. The people in your audience spend time and energy volunteering their time for the causes they care about. If you've done a good job defining your core values, it should be much easier to brandscape your nonprofit involvement.

One brand that's dedicated more than just money to establishing a brandscape with their nonprofit of choice is insurance giant, The Hartford.

Achieve Without Limits

The Hartford is a $21 billion financial services and insurance provider. There are more than 1.5 million people who are part of The Hartford's customer base. On their website, they briefly explain their focused approach to corporate giving:

"Our initiatives in corporate philanthropy extend beyond financial support. We're committed to helping our customers understand and adapt to new, often challenging emotional situations."

The Hartford doesn't highlight tons of charities they contribute to. Instead, they put a huge amount of energy into just one nonprofit that aligns with their core values: the Paralympics.

The Paralympic Games are a series of national and international events where athletes with physical disabilities compete. Paralympic athletes are inspiring. Their stories are emotional. Anyone who knows someone who's suddenly found themselves with a disability understands how emotional and challenging it can be. The Hartford believes you can "achieve without limits." This became the company's corporate tag line for its founding "sponsorship" of the Paralympics.

But they didn't stop with a press release or a logo on the Paralympics website. The Hartford pledged to help raise awareness for the athletes and the games.

"Paralympians are heroes in their own right, but they're also human. Many faced-down formidable challenges to compete before world audiences," reads their website.

The Hartford team started creating unbelievably moving video vignettes featuring the stories of these inspirational athletes. They profiled swimmers and downhill skiers. They told the stories of wheelchair-bound basketball players and one-legged track stars. They even turned these stories into 30-second commercials and aired them on television. These weren't Hartford television spots—they were commercials for achieving without limits. Sure, the commercials featured a Hartford logo, but they weren't about The Hartford's products or services—they were about The Hartford's core values.

The Hartford completely integrated its support for the Paralympics into their social media channels. Some of the campaign ideas seem trivial to me. For example, for each Like they received on Facebook, they donated an additional dollar to the Paralympics (up to 100,000 Likes). Other ideas seemed unbelievably genuine. They invited local Hartford representatives, no matter where they were based, to find Paralympic athletes in their area and share those athletes' stories with their community on Facebook or Twitter.

The Hartford isn't going to move on to another charity next year. They've been working with the Paralympics since 1994. The content they created together was far more effective for both brands than just a cash check or a logo at the event. Together, they created valuable content, shared by both brands, to their respective audiences.

That's a powerful brandscape for a cause.

Tell Their Story

Working with a nonprofit isn't a marketing exercise—it's a commitment to making the world a better place. It doesn't matter if you sponsor the local baseball team or a national nonprofit, if your brand is going to do anything for a nonprofit you should share their stories with your audience.

It will help you emotionally connect with the people who believe in your brand, and it will most certainly raise awareness for the organizations you support.

Any brandscape partnership should be considered a long-term investment in your brand. Nonprofit brandscaping is no different. Instead of showing up once a year to a charity dinner, help your nonprofit show up in your customers' email inboxes and on your Facebook stream. Tell the stories of the people you support.

Brandscaping is about being a good citizen—it's about symbiotic relationships that benefit all the brands involved. Be a good brandscaper: support a nonprofit with content that's valuable to them, not just to you.

27 Questions to Ask Yourself...

Throughout this book, I asked you to "Ask Yourself" one key question in each chapter. Here's a list of those questions. Review it often as you move forward on your brandscaping journey.

1. What products or services do our customers buy before they have a need for our wares?

2. What content does our audience already have a relationship with and how can our brand embrace it?

3. Who already owns our audience?

4. What can we learn from our previous PR hits to prepare for the next one?

5. Who has already authentically embraced our brand?

6. What can we stop doing now to afford ourselves the opportunity to create something of higher value?

7. What expectations have we set for our audience?

8. Where does our audience live online?

9. Who would we want to sing a duet with?

10. What can we do to demonstrate the power of our audience?

11. What are we doing to scale the reach of the people who power our brand?

12. What kind of talent can we work with to make our brand more relevant, more often?

13. What advertisers spend money in the trade magazines our audience reads?

14. How can we package and present our audience with a content brand they can build a relationship with?

15. Can we find a better way to pay for the creation of the content our audience wants from the media brands they trust?

16. How can we experiment with our content brand without investing too much, too fast?

17. Are we treating our content as an asset, or an expense?

18. How can we identify what content is valuable to our audience?

19. What content has successfully garnered our audience's attention in the past?

20. Who can help us brainstorm ideas to devise a good hook?

21. What is the best time for our content to be consumed?

22. Which niche should we go after first?

23. Where can we start to uncover the movements and trends that might move our market?

24. What have we seen, online or off, that might help us identify a content hole?

25. How do we quantify the value of a digital influencer's audience?

26. What is our core value statement?

27. Where should we invest our underwriting dollars?

References

1 Lam, Doug. "Finding Nemo and its Effect on Clownfish in the Wild and in the Aquarium Trade." Nano-Reef.com, April 20, 2009.
http://bit.ly/NxsTjt

2 McCollum, B. A. "Consumer perspectives on the 'web of causality' within the marine aquarium fish trade," Reefbase.org, November 2007.
http://bit.ly/QmA5AH

3 "Kmart goes back to school with second original Web series." RetailingToday.com, August 11, 2011.
http://bit.ly/oZtZT5

4 "What is the cell phone novel?" DailyFig.Figment.com, March 29, 2011.
http://bit.ly/MNqmzM

5 Baldwin, Brad. "4 Responses to 'Blendtec's George Wright on Being the No. 3 Video on YouTube and Getting 5M Hits in 3 Days.'" Podtech.net, November 16, 2006.
http://bit.ly/yR4BS

6 David Meerman Scott has written a wonderful book titled *Newsjacking* (Wiley, 2011). I encourage you to read it.
http://www.davidmeermanscott.com/books/

7 Ingram, Mathew. "How *The Huffington Post* became a new-media behemoth." Gigaom.com, February 2, 2012.
http://bit.ly/zLjvgb

8 Leibach, Sarah. "Look Ma, No Oven! Grilling with George Foreman." College.BigGirlsSmallKitchen.com, April 2011.
http://bit.ly/em1lOD

9 McKenzie, Hamish. "One Man's Email Newsletter Leads the Fight Against Tweet Overload." PandoDaily.com, April 25, 2012.
http://bit.ly/K73bLo

10   "Email Open Rates Up in Q1; Click Rates Drop."
MarketingCharts.com, June 21, 2012.
http://bit.ly/MCdSGb

11   McKenzie, Hamish. "One Man's Email Newsletter Leads the Fight
Against Tweet Overload." PandoDaily.com, April 25, 2012.
http://bit.ly/K73bLo

12   Markowitz, Eric. "Meet the BYU Student Who Took Orabrush Viral."
Inc.com, October 8, 2010.
http://bit.ly/9OOPK7

13   McCracken, Grant. "How Ford Got Social Marketing Right."
Harvard Business Review Blog Network, January 7, 2010.
http://bit.ly/69lt0g

14   On July 9, 2012, Ken Block released the fifth Gymkhana video, shot
on the streets of San Francisco, claiming it's the "ultimate urban
playground." Overnight, the video garnered 8.5 million views propelled by
brandscape partners ranging from X-Games athletes to skateboard
magazine celebs.
http://bit.ly/gymkhana5video

15   Wong, Elaine. "Starbucks Whips Up Frappuccino Campaign."
AdWeek, May 4, 2010.
http://bit.ly/Nxt9Pl

16   Seaman, David. "Who is Jason Sadler, and Why Should You Care?"
Entrepreneur Magazine, September 14, 2009.
http://bit.ly/w6Tmk9

17   Leland, John. "With Studio Space, Musicians Get Sneakers."
New York Times, September 9, 2011.
http://nyti.ms/o73Cml

18   Maloy, Sarah. "Converse's Free Recording Studio, Rubber Tracks,
Opens." Billboard.biz, July 13, 2011.
http://bit.ly/q422LY

19   Leland, John. "With Studio Space, Musicians Get Sneakers."
New York Times, September 9, 2011.
http://nyti.ms/o73Cml

20   Sisario, Ben. "Looking to a Sneaker for a Band's Big Break." *New York Times*, October 6, 2010.
http://nyti.ms/bz6oKC

21   James, Meg. "BofA's influence on U.S. history, as seen on TV." *Los Angeles Times*, April 30, 2010.
http://lat.ms/OqsLyB

22   Newman, Andrew Adam. "A Bank's Ads, Dressed up in Historical Garb." *New York Times,* May 5, 2010.
http://nyti.ms/SWvcvE

23   Lutz, Kristina. "2011 EFFIE Award Review: 'America the Story of Us.'"*Marketing Daily*, June 9, 2011.
http://bit.ly/LQL3vo

24   Ibid.

25   Spaulding, Kameron. "Brew Masters: A show for us beer nuts." Examiner.com, December 6, 2010.
http://exm.nr/P4wNe0

26   Online Brand Value (OBV) is calculated by leveraging Google Insights to track relative search interest over time. Search interest for Dogfish can be seen at:
http://bit.ly/LQL9mD

27   Greenlee, Steve. "Bourdain: Discovery killed 'Brew Masters' because big beer threatened to pull ads." Boston.com, March 30, 2011.
http://bo.st/OfonFV

28   Greenlee, Steve. "Dogfish Head pulling out of RI." Boston.com, March 11, 2011.
http://bo.st/f3eGcA

29   TractorSupply.com, About Tractor Supply

30   InstantWatcher.com, *Fat, Sick & Nearly Dead*, Queued by 1,736 people, April 9, 2012.
http://bit.ly/mgzdhT

31   Compete.com site statistics.

32   Lauby, Sharyn. "7 Considerations for Setting up a Home Office." Workshifting.com, February 2010. http://bit.ly/aovWcw

33   "Survey Finds Organizations Embracing Mobile Workstyles." Citrix Press Release, March 5, 2012. http://bit.ly/xSJJ0p

34   Rooney, Jennifer. "Want to See What Marketing Innovation Looks Like? Go Inside Converse Rubber Tracks With Us." Forbes.com, February 23, 2012. http://onforb.es/wGf2se

35   Creamer, Matthew. "Content: Marketing's Best Hope, or More Hype?" *Advertising Age*, Febuary 27, 2012. http://bit.ly/wrjCdJ

36   IEG Sponsorship Glossary

37   Sprint PCS, PBS.org, NOVA Funders

38   Google, PBS.org, NOVA Funders

39   WaffleShop.org, About The Waffle Shop.

40   A Reality Show, Creativity & The Arts, Carnegie Mellon University. http://bit.ly/MrhGkw

41   "Quaker Oats Launches With New Digital Application Zazu to Help Consumers Get Amazing Start to the Day." Press Release, PepsiCo.com, September 16, 2011. http://bit.ly/qtRcte

Acknowledgments

Anyone who knows me, knows I dream big. I love to look at big problems as the biggest opportunities. I like to make connections and build novel combinations of old ideas leveraging new technology. I take chances, extract the similar from the dissimilar. I like a challenge. Brandscaping is a challenge: a challenge to revolutionize marketing, to reinvent publishing, to expand our thinking about managing talent and the way we inspire consumers to embrace our brands. It's taken me a decade to formulate the ideas you'll find in *Brandscaping*. But I didn't do it alone.

The team at the Content Marketing Institute (and CMI Books) made *Brandscaping* a reality. Joe Pulizzi, who's become a friend over the last five years, encouraged me to take my first speaking engagement and offered me the opportunity to publish my ideas. To Joe, I'm eternally grateful. Lisa Murton Beets took my manuscript and turned it into something special. She's a talented editor and coach. Newt Barrett helped me organize my thoughts, structure my ideas, and made me into a long-form writer—for a guy like me, that's no small feat. To the entire CMI gang including Joseph Kalinowski, Pam Kozelka, Michele Linn, Robert Rose, and Shelly Koenig—thanks to all of you for embracing me as part of the CMI team.

My wife, who married me the year I co-founded Tippingpoint Labs, has supported my every move by encouraging me to write and innovate early in the morning, late at night, and on weekends—her weekends. I owe her a lifetime of gratitude. Her patience and belief in my ultimate success is as steadfast today as it was the day we married.

My mother, Diana (a fellow author) taught me to think big and mentored me as a writer—no, a storyteller. My dad, Jan, encouraged me to fail fast and learn from my mistakes. He motivated me to be the best at whatever I do—and I'm doing it. My father, Roy, has always believed in my ability to succeed even when he's had to put his own resources on the line. I appreciate the investments he and my stepmother, Betty, have made in my business and my education.

My brother, Jonathan (a professional photographer), took my press photos, but he's done much more than that—he's a creative inspiration to anyone who follows their passion. To my brother-in-law, Patrick, I owe a specific debt of gratitude. His persistent early morning calls from the West Coast prodding me to write the next *New York Times* best seller actually made me put my ass in the chair and write everyday. And to my father-in-law, Richard, who taught me everything I know about sales and, whether he knew it or not at the time, sold some of the most innovative brandscapes in the 1970s and 1980s. And to Richard's friend, Jim Demitrieus, whose business advice and constant support has meant a lot to Richard and me both. Thanks to everyone: all my friends and the rest of my extended family for your support. Especially Ryan and Lowry Brescia, Katie and Luis Velez, Sean and Eric Davis, Lindsey King, and Kalie Austin.

Thanks to everyone who's ever worked for, and with, Tippingpoint Labs. Without you my dreams of changing the world wouldn't be possible. My business partner, friend, and best man, James Cosco, has encouraged my big thinking and kept my feet on the ground. Thanks for entertaining my best ideas and discarding, without reservations, the worst. A world of thanks to Brett Virmalo for your loyalty, quick wit, smart thinking, and devotion to the brand. I have the utmost respect for Rebecca Garnick Ast, Bradley Schwarzenbach, Joshua Cole, Anita Roy Dobbs, and Bradley Strauss who've challenged my ideas when they needed it, embraced them when appropriate, and shared them with great gusto and enthusiasm. To Bill Shander, whose partnership and humility has taught me lessons in both life and business. Sean Boice was the first person to read *Brandscaping*, provide feedback, and enhanced the book greatly—you're a wonderful friend. And to others like Nick Jamieson, Robert Collins, Joseph Stucker, Marc Held, and Kevin Dodge who've come through the doors at the 'Labs. You're forever a part of me and the book. Our gratitude must be expressed to all of the clients that have invested in our ideas—especially clients like Breville, TomTom, Putnam Investments, MFS, *The Christian Science Monitor*, and Dell.

To the authors who have inspired, mentored, and coached me—thank you. Brian Massey, David Meerman Scott, C.C. Chapman, and Ann Handley have all made my book a better book, my stories better stories, and my writing better writing.

I interviewed dozens of people in compiling the research for *Brandscaping*. Thanks for taking me seriously, giving freely of your time, and honestly answering my constant queries. A special debt of gratitude is owed to Lauren Luke, Rob Sheard, Mark Malkoff, Mike Lewis, Chris Brogan, Devin Graham, and Bob Sacks.

I've been fortunate enough to have had access to many mentors over the last three decades. People like Claude Pelanne and Dean Gaskill taught me how to succeed in the media business. Peter van Roden helped me understand how to manage creative people. Eugene Wu helped me learn how to run a startup. To those mentors who took the time to read my book (in its most raw and unedited form), my deepest gratitude: Bob Sacks, Jeff Carter, Mike O'Toole, Steve Rotter, Cathy Perron, and Brian Massey. I'd be remiss if I didn't thank my high school friend, Richard Yoo, for believing in my big ideas enough that he introduced me to Morris Miller, who gave me the push I needed, when I needed it, to put pen on paper.

To all of you who've embraced my creative spirit and inspired my thinking, thank you. This book is as much yours as it is mine.

About Andrew M. Davis

Andrew Davis' inspirational, unconventional, and sometimes controversial concepts are a product of his diverse life and business experiences. His childhood acting career provided the training ground that makes him a highly-engaging and entertaining speaker at trade shows, conferences, and corporate events around the world.

Andrew's past experiences as a television writer and producer have contributed to his theories on how to build a relationship with a valuable audience through the generation of great content powered by exceptional talent. He honed his marketing and product-development skills during the first dot-com boom, which shaped his business-oriented approach to driving real revenue and results. Finally, his co-founding of Tippingpoint Labs, led to the practical fusion of his varied experiences servicing brands that sell everything from consumer products to subscriptions.

Andrew got his start in the media business at a young age appearing in television commercials and voicing over radio spots for brands like Cadbury, Chevrolet, Six Flags, and McDonalds. By middle school, he'd started his first business—a magic and marionette show for kids—while he performed in operas and musicals with stars like Dame Joan Sutherland and *Dukes of Hazard* star, John Schneider.

After graduating from Boston University's College of Communication with a degree in Television and Film (and a minor in philosophy), Andrew stepped behind the camera, and off the stage, to start producing call-in, public affairs programming at a local television station. From there he helped support the growth of the cable news network explosion by joining VideoLink, producing segments for NBC's *Today Show*, CNN, *Fox News*, CNBC, the BBC, and many more. It's there that he had the opportunity to pitch, write, and produce segments for television icon Charles Kuralt's syndicated program, *American Moments*.

Andrew chased his dream job to New York and landed as the production manager in the Muppet workshop for the Jim Henson company, helping contribute to the success of television shows (including *Sesame Street* and *Bear in the Big Blue House*) and films (including *Muppets From Space* and *Elmo in Grouchland*). The technology boom in the late 1990s sparked his interest in new media and he road the wave through startups that included The Stock Market Photo Agency, ThinkAgent Technologies, and Sallie Mae Solutions, filling roles that ranged from marketing to product development.

In 2001, Andrew and his business partner, James Cosco, founded Tippingpoint Labs. Jim's television background and training as a journalist, combined with Andrew's media, technology, and marketing expertise, led to the acquisition of clients including financial services, consumer packaged-goods, publishers, and technology brands.

As chief strategy officer at Tippingpoint Labs, Andrew rallies his team to change the way content creators think, authentic talent is nurtured, and companies market their products. When he's not at their Boston headquarters, he's traveling the globe sharing his insight, experience, stories, and optimistic ideals through his wildly fascinating speaking engagements.

If you've made it all the way through this bio and want to learn more about Andrew or tap into his creative approach to almost anything, track him down at www.brandscapingbook.com/speaking, follow him on Twitter @tpldrew, or call him at (617) 286-4009. He'll be glad you did.

Have Andrew Speak at Your Next Event

Andrew Davis is available for keynote presentations and full-day seminars. He is a frequent speaker at trade shows, conferences, and corporate events around the world.

Andrew's sessions have been described as "theatrical, dazzling, and inspiring." He's a big thinker, and an innovator who sees opportunity at every turn. Andrew infuses his presentations with a unique blend of humor, history, and storytelling designed to inspire audiences to rethink their marketing, sales, even entire industries, by leveraging the right kind of digital partnerships that drive business. For more than a decade, he's led the charge to change the way publishers think and how brands market their products in a digital world covering topics ranging from social media to ecommerce and even the future of publishing.

Visit www.brandscapingbook.com/speaking for more information about speaking packages that include copies of *Brandscaping*, and to see Andrew in action.

Discounted Book Copies and Free Brainstorming Sessions

It is my hope that *Brandscaping* has helped change the way you think about marketing and growing your business. But, chances are, you can't do it alone. I understand that, so I've done my best to find ways to help you share Brandscaping with others. At www.brandscapingbook.com/packages you'll have access to discounted copies of the book and even access to packages that include free brainstorming sessions with me and your team. Let me help you spread the idea that a rising tide lifts all ships.

Interactive Reference Guide

There are hundreds of references to web resources, ideas, examples, case studies, and people in *Brandscaping*. Sure, you can use a search engine to find them all, but I've taken the time to compile an interactive companion iBook that includes many of the videos, screenshots, examples, and even case studies into an affordable resource and reference for those interested in taking a deeper dive. It is my hope that they serve as an inspiration and resource for you and your colleagues as you start thinking as a brandscaper. You can find more information about *Brandscaping: A Reference Guide* at www.brandscapingbook.com/reference. There, you'll also find information about discounted packages of books for your team that include free consulting or in-person lectures with me.

Interactive Teacher's Resource

I believe that it's a new generation of business leaders, marketing executives, talent managers, and agency principals that will truly be able to harness the power of brandscaping to build businesses in new and inventive ways. That's why I've created a companion iBook as a teacher's resource for *Brandscaping*. The interactive book is full of challenges, project ideas, questions, and discussion topics designed to fuel creative thinking in higher education classrooms around the world. You can find more information about *Brandscaping: A Teacher's Resource* at www.brandscapingbook.com/teachers. There, you'll find information about discounted packages of books for your classroom that include Skype sessions or in-person lectures with me.

More Praise for *Brandscaping*...

Gamechanging!

"*Brandscaping* crystallizes the very complex issues facing marketers today with an amazing blend of home-run success stories, in the trenches insight, and an optimistic challenge for every business leader to ask: 'what if?'"

> — *Steve Rotter, vice president of marketing, Brightcove, and technology entrepreneur*

Fast-paced blueprint...

"Are you spending boatloads of money to buy attention through advertising? How's that working for you? Andrew Davis shows you a better way—brandscaping—the art and science of earning attention in a crowded world by publishing content that gets people interested and talking about you. *Brandscaping* is no mere academic theory. It's a fast-paced blueprint chock full of examples of success to learn from."

> — *David Meerman Scott, bestselling author of **The New Rules of Marketing and PR**, now in over 25 languages from Bulgarian to Vietnamese*

Dozens of great stories...

"Brandscaping is a refreshingly big idea, one that holds the promise of redefining tired notions of paid and earned media, branded content, and editorial content. Andrew Davis shares dozens of great stories of companies that have grown their markets by forming unconventional partnerships to create content their audiences can't get enough of."

> — *Mike O'Toole, president and partner, PJA Advertising*

You must read this book!

"Filled with common-sense solutions that sometimes elude us all, *Brandscaping* enables you to leverage your content as an asset instead of an expense. It arms you with a new way of thinking about a still evolving digital age."

— *Bob Sacks, president, Precision Media Group*

An intellectual adventure and a practical guide...

"*Brandscaping* is one of the few business books that's both an intellectual adventure and a practical guide. Andrew Davis' entertaining case studies and novel ideas bring new life to established marketing traditions with a singular vision that's often difficult for most of us to see. You hold in your hands a solid marketing blueprint designed specifically to impact and accelerate your sales pipeline in the digital age. Let your brandscaping adventure begin!"

— *Nick Patrissi, national director, Marketing & Business Development, Trend Offset Printing*

Finally a framework...

"There are thousands of ways to put content marketing to work in our businesses. Finally, we have a framework with which to implement content of all kinds—the brandscape. Chock full of examples, *Brandscaping* architects the process of reaching out to prospects and customers with a consistent eye toward growing our brands and businesses. This is a must-read for any modern marketer."

— *Brian Massey, The Conversion Scientist™, author of* ***Your Customer Creation Equation***

A must read for marketing professionals…

"Andrew Davis has done a terrific job deconstructing an increasingly complicated new media landscape. *Brandscaping* is a must-read for marketing professionals, entrepreneurs, and content producers. The strategies in this book offer anyone innovative opportunities to leverage valuable content that brings your brand (and your partners) to the forefront of the marketplace. Get ready to pave the way for a new total-product experience—one that ensures consumer loyalty with staying power."

— Cathy Perron, director, Media Ventures Program,
Boston University College of Communication

Content Marketing Institute Titles

Managing Content Marketing
The Real-World Guide for Creating Passionate Subscribers to Your Brand
By Robert Rose & Joe Pulizzi

Capturing Community
How to Build, Manage, and Market Your Online Community
By Michael Silverman

Bold Brand
The New Rules for Differentiating, Branding, and Marketing Your Professional Services Firm
By Josh Miles

Your Customer Creation Equation
Unexpected Website Formulas of the Conversion Scientist™
By Brian Massey

Brandscaping
Unleashing the Power of Partnerships
By Andrew M. Davis

The Marketer's Guide to SlideShare
How to Build Your Brand, Generate Leads & Create Opportunities
By Todd Wheatland

Content Marketing Institute books are available at special quantity discounts to use as premiums and sales promotions, or for use in corporate training programs. To place a bulk order, please contact the Content Marketing Institute at info@contentinstitute.com or 888/554-2014.

www.contentmarketinginstitute.com

CPSIA information can be obtained
at www.ICGtesting.com
Printed in the USA
BVHW04215305012 0
568539BV00007B/10/P

9 780983 330783